THE HATFIELDS
& THE MCCOYS

THE HATFIELDS
& THE MCCOYS

BRUCE WEXLER

Skyhorse Publishing

Copyright ©2013 Pepperbox Press Ltd.
First published in the United States in 2013
by Skyhorse Publishing, Inc.
All Rights Reserved. No part of this book
may be reproduced in any manner without
the express written consent of the publisher,
except in the case of brief excerpts in critical
reviews or articles. All inquiries should be
addressed to
Skyhorse Publishing, 555 Eighth Avenue,
Suite 903, New York, NY 10018.
Skyhorse Publishing books may be
purchased in bulk at special discounts for
sales promotion, corporate gifts, fund-raising,
or educational purposes. Special editions
can also be created to specifications. For
details, contact the Special Sales Department,
Skyhorse Publishing, 555 Eighth Avenue,
Suite 903, New York, NY 10018 or
info@skyhorsepublishing.com.
www.skyhorsepublishing.com

10 9 8 7 6 5 4 3 2

Library of Congress Cataloging-in-
Publication
Data is available on file.

2013 Edition printed for
Barnes & Noble, Inc.
ISBN: 978-1-4351-4525-2

Printed in China

CONTENTS

FOREWORD

I F A SINGLE FAMILY DISPUTE has captured the American imagination, it must be the feud between the Hatfields and the McCoys. When the families first fell out in the 1860s it was against the backdrop of the Civil War. Traumatic wartime experiences deeply affected the patriarchs of both families and their rift seemed to reflect the national struggle. By the time the feud subsided in the 1890s it had resulted in at least twelve deaths and many more broken lives. It left bitter wounds that were not fully healed for over a century.

The feud itself seemed to be about almost nothing, but the personalities involved kept it at boiling point for nearly thirty years. Hatfield-McCoy violence pulsed along the Tug Valley region in waves and affected hundreds of participants. Each pulse reflected a traumatic event in the lives of one or other of the families and resulted from a seemingly unquenchable thirst for revenge. Its victims included women, children, and the impaired, although men in their prime were also snuffed out.

The violence was so intense and fearful that it served to further isolate the Appalachian country and exclude it from the

Left: Three McCoy relatives. Left to right: Syler Branham, J.E. Stanley, and Joe Jack Stanley Jr..

Left: Hatfield family members on the homestead porch.

progress being experienced by the rest of the nation. The ever-present fear of violence held the region back for decades. The railroad stayed away and the area's natural resources remained unexploited.

Why has this particular feud become part of the American story? It was not the worst family feud in history, as others claimed more lives. It was not the longest feud as others rumbled on for over a century. Perhaps it was the extraordinarily complex characters that fought in it, each one part hero and part villain. Whatever it is, the Hatfield–McCoy feud has become an intrinsic part of the national legend, a footnote from a past age of violent self-expression.

THE ORIGINS OF THE CLANS

Previous pages:
Originally, the McCoy
clan came from the
Scottish Lowlands.

IF FAMILY CLANNISHNESS was one of root causes of the Hatfield-McCoy feud, the very origins of the families themselves were part of the problem.

The Origins of the McCoys

The McCoy clan originally came from the Lowlands of Scotland, but gradually re-located to the Scotland's Sutherland Highlands. McCoy family members intermarried with Celts from this wild and beautiful region in the north. Life in this sparsely populated terrain was very tough, and local families survived by sticking together. Highland McCoys were notoriously tall and handsome, with olive complexions and dark or auburn hair. The clan crest and motto, "Manu Forti" or "With a strong hand" indicates both strength and a warlike attitude. The blue-and-gold family crest features a suit of armor, two daggers, three silver bears' heads, and a buck's head.

Despite their strength, life in the harsh terrain of northern Scotland proved too difficult for even the McCoys. By 1700, the family had joined over one hundred thousand Scottish Protestants who crossed the twelve miles of open sea between Scotland and Ireland in search of a better life. This migration had been encouraged by James I (the first king of a unified Scotland and England) at the beginning of the seventeenth century as a means of colonizing Roman Catholic Ireland with "loyal" Scottish Protestants. James's English subjects were generally unwilling to make the trek to this far-flung outpost of the British Isles. But the Scots were living under much more difficult economic conditions, and were more willing to emigrate. Ironically, James I tried to limit this migration to Lowland Scots, as he considered the Scottish Highlanders far too wild and unruly, like the Irish themselves.

Under the influence of these Scottish migrants, the northern part of Ireland became an economic success. The first recorded McCoy, the Jacobite John McCoy, immigrated to County Antrim in the northern part of Ireland in 1715, accompanied by his brothers James and Daniel. (Jacobites were supporters of the deposed British King James II.) The McCoys finally left Scotland after a failed attempt to re-establish the Catholic Stuart dynasty as the royal house of Britain. Once in Ireland, the family worked for Sir Marcus Beresford. Beresford was ennobled by George I in

Following pages: By the beginning of the nineteenth century, the Hatfields and the McCoys were both living in the Tug Valley.

1720 and became a member of the Irish House of Lords.

But with the introduction of the Test Act in 1704, conditions in Ireland began to decline. The Test Act excluded Scots-Irish Catholics and Presbyterians from public office, and deprived their clergy of their legal standing. A toxic combination of religious persecution, bad harvests, a recession in the Irish linen industry, and high rent increases led to over a quarter of a million Scots-Irish leaving the country. The McCoys joined this wave of immigration from the port of Belfast and arrived in America in 1732. At this time, America was becoming increasingly populous, with an immigrant population of over 1.5 million. The young nation was by now a mostly Anglophone country.

John McCoy's son Archibald, the first American member of the family, was born in Washington County, Maryland on July 12, 1732. John had four more American-born sons, David, William, Joel, and John Jr. Five years later he was awarded a land grant of 150 acres in Charles County, Maryland, located just outside the township of Funkstown. In 1742 John bought a further fifty acres in Prince George's County, Maryland. This parcel of land was known as Neglect. McCoy continued to purchase property and in January 1748 bought 129 acres in Queen Anne County, Maryland followed by a further tract of fifty-four acres in Charles County, Maryland in 1747. This land was known as Slatford's Roost Extension. From this pattern of land acquisition, we can see that the McCoy family was becoming both settled and prosperous, and that their family fortune was based in property.

Ultimately John McCoy became a prominent landowner, and this fact was destined to become especially significant. On his death in 1762, his property was divided between his sons. The eldest son, Archibald McCoy, inherited the Neglect property, complete with an elegant stone mansion that his father had built and lived in. Archibald married a woman called Elizabeth Blair in 1751 and the couple went on to have an extensive family of twelve children: William, John, James, Rachel, Mary, Susannah, Lavinia, Lydia, Elizabeth, Nancy, Archibald, and Edmund. The children were born between 1752 and 1776. Almost all of them survived long enough to have large families of their own, generating an increasingly large and successful clan of American McCoys. It was the couple's eldest son, William McCoy, who was to become the progenitor of the notorious McCoys of legend. He was known in the clan as "Old William." In 1772, William married Cordelia Campbell of Giles, Virginia. The couple had a large brood of thirteen children who were born between 1773 and the early years of the nineteenth century. The 1790 United States Federal Census places they as living in North Milford in Cecil County, Maryland but the family subsequently moved to Montgomery County, Virginia. Several of their children were born there. During the Revolution, William served in the Virginia Continental Army and was awarded a

Following pages: A famous family portrait of the Hatfield clan. Front row left to right: Tennis Hatfield, Levisa Hatfield (Johnse's daughter), Willis Hatfield, and Yellow Watch (Devil Anse's coon and bear dog).
Second row: Mrs. Mary Hensley-Simpkins-Howes (Devil Anse's daughter), Devil Anse Hatfield, Levisa Chafin Hatfield, Nancy Elizabeth Hatfield (Cap's wife), Robert Elliott Hatfield (Cap's son), Louise Hatfield (Cap's daughter), Cap Hatfield, and Coleman Hatfield (Cap's son).
Top row: Rosa Lee Hatfield (Devil Anse's daughter), Troy Hatfield, Betty Hatfield Caldwell (Devil Anse's daughter), Elias Hatfield, Tom Chafin, Joe D. Hatfield, Ock Damron, Shephard Hatfield (Cap's son), Levisa Emma Hatfield (Cap's daughter), and Bill Border.

war bounty voucher for his loyal service. The voucher was for two hundred acres of land, located in Floyd and Pike Counties, Kentucky.

The McCoys finally arrived in the Tug Valley in 1794, when William settled at Gulnare in Pike County, Kentucky. Six of William McCoy's sons settled nearby on both the Kentucky and West Virginia sides of the Tug River, a tributary of the Big Sandy River. The Tug Valley runs between the Great Appalachian Valley and the Ohio River. The four remaining sons continued on their way westwards.

The Tug Valley was to play a major role in the history of the McCoy family, and many McCoy descendants still call the area home. The valley had first been explored in the 1790s by Robin and Steve Hensley. The Hensleys were mountain men who came to the area hunting bear. Part of their hunting kit included deer hide "tugs" that they used to tie around the bearskins so that they could carry them. A terrible drought struck while the pair was hunting in the area, and they were forced to stew and eat the tugs to survive. The Hensleys named the valley the "Tug" in honor of their survival.

The Tug Valley was gradually settled. The incoming population established a mixed economy of farming, hunting, and harvesting forest resources. Coal mining also became an important local industry. The valley is now dotted with quaint little towns including

Williamson, Matewan, Gilbert, Delbarton, Kermit, and South Williamson.

William McCoy appeared in the 1810 census of Floyd County, Kentucky. William and the six sons who settled the area all became prosperous, but the couple's fourth son Samuel McCoy (born in 1792) built up land holdings of around fifteen hundred acres around the Tug River. Samuel and his wife Elizabeth Davis went on to have eighteen children who were born between 1803 and 1839.

It was the subsequent generation that became embroiled in the feud with the Hatfield family. Samuel's son Benjamin, born in 1820, married his cousin Phoebe McCoy in 1839 and had three children with her: John, Ellen, and Ulysses. Phoebe died, leaving her husband to raise their children alone, and Benjamin remarried in 1851. His second wife was Nancy Robinette, the daughter of a local family. Between 1852 and 1879, the couple had fourteen more children.

Samuel's sister Sarah, or Sally, McCoy married another McCoy cousin in 1849. Her husband was to become the clan patriarch Randolph, or Old Randall McCoy. Born in 1825 in Pike County, Kentucky, Randolph McCoy was to become a pivotal figure in the Hatfield-McCoy feud. Between 1848 and 1873 Randall and Sally had sixteen children: Joseph, James, Floyd, Tolbert, Samuel, Lilburn, Alifair, Rosanna, Calvin, Pharmer, Randolph, William, Trinvilla, Adelaide, Fanny, and Mary. Several of the McCoy children were to lose their lives in the course of the notorious feud.

The Origins of the Hatfields

The Hatfield family came from Hatfield in South Yorkshire, England, several hundred miles further south than the McCoys. Before England became a united country, Hatfield was the scene of a deadly battle in 633 between the forces of King Edwin of Deira and King Penda of Mercia.

The first known Hatfield, Bede de Hatfield, was born in East Hatfield in 1139. His great grandson Walter became a baron. The family flourished around various towns in Yorkshire and Derbyshire. For a few generations, the family name mutated to Hetfelde, but was restored to Hatfield by the middle of the sixteenth century. John Hetfelde was born in Hatfield, Yorkshire in 1539. The son of John and Anne Hetfelde, John was a successful merchant who travelled abroad for his work. By this time, the family was established in Almondbury, a small village in the West Riding region of Yorkshire, England. The village was catalogued as Almondberie in 1086's *Domesday Book.* The book was King William I's attempt to value the kingdom of England and Wales for tax purposes. Several Hatfields appeared in the document.

By Tudor times, Almondbury was an active commercial center with merchants dealing in wool, silk, and coal. It is very likely that the Hatfield family was attracted to the town by its trading activities. John Hatfield was born in Almondbury in 1563. He married Elizabeth Bright and his son Johis Hatfield was born in 1589. By this time the Hatfields had become Dissenters, Protestants who had left the established Church of England because they felt its services and liturgy were becoming too close to the Roman Catholic Church. The British monarchy saw these independent-minded individuals as a threat to its authority. When James I came to the throne in 1603, he proceeded to introduce repressive legislation that was designed to keep Dissenters out of public office and make it difficult for them to earn a living. This was the very same legislation that was to lead to the McCoys leaving Scotland for the New World.

Thomas Hatfield was born in Almondbury in the early 1600s. He worked in the local wool trade as a young man, but soon felt the need to leave England to avoid religious persecution. In 1620, he went to join Dr. John Robinson's congregation in the university town of Leiden in Holland. Robinson was to become known as the inspiration of the Pilgrim Fathers. He instituted a communal way of living for his followers who lived together in a large house called the Grone Point. In 1620, thirty-five members of Robinson's community sailed to the New World on the *Mayflower*, but neither Robinson himself nor Thomas Hatfield joined the party. Robinson, who was noted for his "broadly tolerant mind," died in Leiden in 1625.

In 1621 Thomas Hatfield married Anna Hentem Cox in

Leiden, Holland. The couple's son Mattias Hatfield was born in Danzig, Poland on August 25, 1640. It was Mattias Hatfield who was to take his family to America in the 1660s.

When the Hatfields arrived in the New World, America was in a state of flux. In 1664 British forces seized the Dutch colonies. Fort Orange became Albany and New Amsterdam became New York. Immigration from Britain had increased as many people tried to escape religious conformity and bad economic conditions.

In 1664 Mattias Hatfield married Maria Melyn (Melen or Moylen) in New Haven, Connecticut. Between 1666 and 1676 Mattias and Maria had six children, including Abraham Hatfield who was born in 1670. Mattias and his family settled in Elizabethtown in Essex County, New Jersey and he quickly became a luminary of the town. The family owned tanneries on the Elizabeth River. In 1673 Mattias bought a stone house on Pearl Street in Elizabethtown, at the corner of Hatfield. This property extended down to the river and remained in the family until the twentieth century. Mattias donated a piece of ground on which to build the town's Presbyterian Church and burial ground. He also sat as a chosen freeholder in the town's court and was a justice, high sheriff, and a collector for the county.

Abraham Hatfield followed his father into the leather business and ran a tannery with his brother Cornelius. He was also a cordwainer, or shoemaker. Abraham married a woman named

Phoebe Ogden and they had eight children together, including Abraham Jr. who was born in Elizabethtown in 1695. Abraham Jr. and his wife Margaret Winans had several children, including George Goff Hatfield who was born in 1715. The couple both survived until 1745, when they died in Elizabethtown, New Jersey.

It was George Hatfield who made the move to Virginia. Virginia was considered a settled area of America, living peacefully under British control. In the following years, the Hatfield family gradually moved westwards to the West Virginian side of the Appalachian Mountains. George Hatfield appeared on a list of tax payers for Botecourt County, Virginia, but was to become one of the early pioneers to settle along the Clinch River in southwest Virginia. George also appeared on Robert Doach's muster list for the Clinch River district. He and his wife Marthy Toms had several children, including Joseph Hatfield Jr. who was born around 1739 or 1740 in Isle of Wight County, Virginia. Joseph married Elizabeth Deliz Vance in 1760. Joseph Hatfield served as a private during the Revolutionary War and as an Indian scout and spy. Joseph and Elizabeth Hatfield had five children, including the notorious Ephraim "Eaf of All" Hatfield, named for Elizabeth's father. Ephraim was born in 1765 or 1756 in Washington County, Virginia, and Alexander ("Ale") followed in 1778. Elizabeth died at the age of forty-three in 1778, and Joseph remarried a woman called Rachel Smith. Joseph himself died at the great age of

Right: Randolph or Randall McCoy was born on October 30, 1825 in the Tug River Valley, Kentucky. He died on March 28, 1914 in Pikeville, Kentucky. Randall was the patriarch of the McCoy family during the Hatfield-McCoy feud.

ninety-three in 1832 in Campbell County, Tennessee. Strangely, Joseph's son Ephraim married his father's second wife's sister Mary Polly Smith in Russell County, Virginia in 1785. Both women were the daughters of Ericus Smith and his wife Brigitta Anderson Andersdatter.

Ephraim Hatfield's first marriage produced five children: Joseph, Eli, Ericus, Valentine (known as "Wall" and born in Russell County, Virginia in 1789), and Lydian Bridget. His second marriage to the widow Anna McKinney Musick Bundy in 1830 produced six more children: Mary Polly, George, Margaret, Jeremiah, Anna, and Phoebe. Ephraim died in 1847 in Blackberry Creek, Pike County, Kentucky.

Ephraim's son Wall Hatfield married Martha Weddington and the couple produced nine sons and three daughters, including Ephraim ("Big Eaf") Hatfield who was born in 1811. The family lived in Logan County, Virginia at the Hatfield place at Horsepen. Wall's brother Joseph lived nearby at Matewan. Wall's children and their descendants colonized the area by marrying into well-known and influential families and the Hatfields became increasingly prominent. Their influence was felt in trade, timber, and law enforcement. Strangely, although it was Wall's grandchildren who were to become the "feuding" generation of the Hatfield clan, he himself was known as a peaceable and quiet man who served as a justice of the peace.

Left: Randall married his first cousin Sarah McCoy on December 9, 1849. The couple settled down on a three-hundred-acre farm in Pike County, Kentucky and went on to have sixteen children together. Their children were named Josephine, James, Floyd, Tolbert, Lilburn, Samuel, Mary, Alifair, Roseanna, Calvin, Pharmer, Bud, William, Trinvilla, Adelaide, and Fannie.

Previous pages:
The West Virginian
town of Matewan
photographed in
1908.

Wall's son Ephraim ("Big Eaf") married Nancy (or Bette Vance) and produced a reputed eighteen children of his own. These included Valentine ("Uncle Wall," born in 1834), Martha who was born in 1838, William Anderson ("Devil Anse," born on September 9, 1839 in Logan, West Virginia), Ellison (who was to marry Nancy McCoy's daughter), and Elias ("Good Lias," who was born in 1848). Like Ellison, a child of Wall's generation, Jeremiah's son Ephraim also married a McCoy girl, Elizabeth, and his grandson Johnson married Nancy McCoy.

Big Eaf's son William Anderson ("Devil Anse") was to become the patriarch of the Hatfield family, although Wall was the eldest son. Devil Anse was raised in the rugged Appalachian Mountains of southwest Virginia. As a boy, he loved to hunt black bears and was known as one of the best horsemen and marksmen of the area. It was a skill he was to retain all his life. William Anderson Hatfield married Levisa Chafin on April 18, 1861 in Logan County, West Virginia. The couple raised thirteen children who were born between 1862 and 1890. They were named Johnson (Johnse), William (Cap), Robert E. Lee, Nancy, Elliott, Mary, Elizabeth, Elias, Detroit (Troy), Joseph, Rosie, Emmanuel Wilson (Willis), and Tennyson (Tennis).

Left: Devil Anse loved
to hunt black bears
and was known
as one of the best
marksmen in the
rugged Appalachian
Mountains.

Although he was illiterate, Devil Anse Hatfield was known as a witty man. He was tall, strong, and wiry, weighing around 175 pounds. He had brown eyes and was known to be very proud of his full head of hair and chest-length beard. He and his family lived at Tug Fork but moved to Thacker Creek, West Virginia in 1888 when the wearisome feud was over. Devil Anse was also an aggressive businessman who made his living from farming, timber, and real estate. He was also notorious for vigorously defending his interests. This aggressive protectionism was not to augur well for the Hatfield family.

The Scene is Set

By the middle of the nineteenth century both the Hatfields and the McCoys had arrived at the feuding generations.

It is interesting to note that the histories of the two families mirrored each other very closely. Both families were non-conformist Protestants who were forced to leave Great Britain to avoid religious persecution and social relegation. Although they could have either abandoned their beliefs, or simply accepted the difficulties of their situations, both families chose to emigrate rather than bow to authority.

Both families were part of early waves of immigration to America (the Hatfields had had the opportunity to migrate on the *Mayflower* with other members of their sect). Having arrived in the New World, later generations of both families gravitated westwards to Virginia's Appalachian mountain region around the Tug River

Right: A sketch of a mountain feud. Feuding became synonymous with the Appalachian region during the nineteenth century. It took almost a further century for this image to be erased from the public imagination.

Valley. Both families subsequently became involved in the local timber industry and began to acquire land and property. Both the Hatfields and the McCoys flourished, with many children being born into the family in each generation. As a result, both clans became extensive. Together they began to dominate the region.

The Hatfields were more materially successful than the McCoys, but both of the families produced flocks of healthy children. Their descendants intermarried and lived peacefully alongside each other for several generations. Both families were strong, loyal, and ambitious.

But despite this outward appearance of normality, something was wrong in the makeup of both families. For the moment this lay dormant. This something was a terrible spark of violence that, when the right conditions arose, would ignite into an inferno. The two families were to engage in one of the most notorious family feuds in American history and many of them were to lose their lives because of it.

Right: Family feuding became a bitter aspect of Appalachian life. The very real danger to outsiders held the region back for decades.

APPALACHIA: THE CRADLE OF THE FEUD

APPALACHIA NOT ONLY PROVIDED a dramatic background to this notorious feud, but the traditions and conditions of the region also fanned the flames of the Hatfield-McCoy conflagration.

Appalachia is far larger than many people imagine. It is a mountainous region that sprawls across thirteen states in the east of the United States, from Alabama in the south to New York in the north. It covers over two hundred thousand square miles. Appalachia is now home to over twenty-three million people, but even today pockets of the region can feel isolated. In the past, the remoteness of this beautiful mountainous land generated a unique cultural tradition.

The earliest Appalachian settlers were Native American hunter-gatherers who arrived over twelve thousand years ago. The first European settlers arrived in the late seventeenth century and found the Shawnee and Cherokee tribes living in the area. Appalachia is the fourth oldest surviving European place name in the United States. Spanish cartographers named the mountains in the early sixteenth century. As European immigrants gradually colonized Virginia and the Carolinas, they gradually pushed west in the Appalachian Mountains. Like the Hatfields and McCoys, ninety percent of these new settlers came from the Anglo-Scottish border country: the English counties of Cumberland, Westmoreland, Northumberland, Durham, Lancashire, and Yorkshire, and the Scottish counties of Ayrshire, Dumfrieshire, Roxburghshire, and Berwickshire. It is noticeable that, to this day, the Appalachian dialect has a strong Scottish influence, quite unlike most American accents. Technically, this is known as the Southern Midland dialect. The remaining European immigrants came to the region from Ireland, Wales, Switzerland, and Germany.

Once Thomas Walker had crossed the Cumberland Gap in 1750, settlers were able to reach the heart of Appalachia for the first time. Due to its isolated nature, this newly-explored region was known as the backcountry. The Native American tribes of the region were gradually driven out by the incomers, culminating in the tragic Trail of Tears of 1838. By this time almost all the Appalachian Cherokees had been driven from the region. This terrible event brought an end to clashes between the indigenous Native Americans and the European settlers.

Although one source of conflict was ended, Appalachia was still considered to be a wild and uncivilized area beyond the reach of the law. This view was reinforced by the fact that most early Appalachians were self-reliant hunters and frontiersmen who did not cooperate with authority. These men were epitomized by the rugged and self-sufficient pioneer Daniel Boone. Dressed in his buckskin jacket and coonskin cap and armed with his long rifle and powder horn, Boone was one of the original mountain men. These were the first white men to live in the Appalachian Mountains.

These hardy pioneers soon gained a reputation for independent thinking and living. They often found themselves at odds with the authorities that sought to tax and control them. Many mountain men became involved in the North Carolina Regulator Movement in the mid-eighteenth century. The Regulators objected to the harsh taxes levied on the region's country folk and farmers by a wealthy and powerful minority of educated incomers. The extravagant governor's mansion built by Governor William Tryon became a focus of local resentment as higher taxes were levied to pay for it. But although their cause was just, some Appalachian wild men used the movement as an excuse for violence and vandalism. On the other hand, many Regulators went on to become part of the American Revolution that took place between 1775 and 1783 and became influential at a national level.

Most Appalachians were determined not to be governed from

Right: The handsome Ellison Hatfield wears his Confederate uniform and carries his Colt Army revolver. Ellison fought for the Confederacy for the duration of the Civil War.

afar by men who knew nothing about their way of life. Many Appalachians became pivotal in the Illinois Campaign of 1779. They were led by George Rogers Clark, a major in Virginia's Kentucky County Militia. The main action of the campaign took place in Illinois County, Virginia, where Clark's forces helped to drive out the occupying British forces from the region. In this way, Appalachian men became instrumental in breaking the political grip of the British and French on the northwestern United States. In the following year, the Overmountain Men of the western Appalachian Mountains were crucial in the defeat of the British forces at the Battle of Kings Mountain in York County, South Carolina.

The Whiskey Rebellion

Left: Asa Harmon McCoy was the only member of the feuding families to fight for the Union during the Civil War. He enlisted as a private in Company E of the 45th Kentucky Mounted Infantry. He was murdered in 1865, leaving a widow and six fatherless children, including Nancy McCoy Hatfield Phillips.

But the dismissal of the British did not mean that the Appalachian people were happy to pay heavy taxes imposed by their new domestic rulers. The Whiskey Rebellion of 1791 broke out when the Appalachian grain farmers refused to pay a special tax on the whiskey they distilled from their spare grain. Whiskey was particularly important to the economy of the region as it was easier to transport over the poor mountain roads than bulky grain was. Appalachian farmers particularly resented paying taxes to state legislators who refused to reinvest in the region, effectively draining Appalachia of its resources. The whiskey levy meant that Appalachians were taxed more harshly than their eastern counterparts who farmed much less challenging terrain and didn't need to distill moonshine whiskey to make a living. These small scale distillers were also taxed more steeply than the commercial whiskey makers of the East who were taxed at the same flat rate but produced far more. The whiskey tax became a focus for general discontent and two whiskey tax collectors were attacked in 1791. Resistance hardened to such an extent that it became a threat to the federal government itself and many people from the region believed that they would be better off as a separate state. The situation descended into outright armed resistance in 1783's Battle of Bower Hill. The rebellion was forcefully suppressed, but it had shown that many American citizens did not recognize the ultimate authority of the federal government and believed that all citizens had the innate right to challenge the government.

By the 1830s disaffected Appalachians had begun to support the new Whig party, established to oppose President Andrew Jackson and his Democratic party. Whigs were generally viewed as pro-liberty and anti-tyranny. Abraham Lincoln was the leading member of the Whig party in frontier Illinois. The party had been formed in opposition to 1828's Tariff of Abominations. These were taxes levied on imports to the United States. This regime of protectionist tariffs greatly benefitted the manufacturing states of

Right: Asa Harmon McCoy was the brother of McCoy patriarch Randall McCoy.

the North, but hugely raised the cost of living in the South.

The Civil War in Appalachia

During the Civil War, Appalachia was bitterly divided by the issue of slavery. The north of the region was mostly pro-abolitionist, while most southern Appalachians wanted to retain the *status quo*. The region effectively mirrored the political schism of the nation and many violent battles took place on its soil as the war raged. The Shenandoah Valley of Virginia and the city of Chattanooga, Tennessee were particularly affected by the conflict. The Shenandoah was known as the breadbasket of the Confederacy and was also an area from where Confederate troops launched attacks on the Union states of Maryland, Washington, and Pennsylvania. This drew down the full vengeance of the Union forces on the valley and three devastating campaigns were fought there. The Valley Campaign of 1862 to 1864 was led by Union general Philip Sheridan, who finally broke the Confederate forces with his infamous scorched earth policy. In 1863 Chattanooga was bombarded and occupied by the Union forces of Ulysses S. Grant.

Despite these famous engagements, Appalachia did not suffer as much from the regular armies on both sides as it did from the notorious bushwhackers that plagued the region. Bushwhackers were irregular troops from both sides of the conflict who used extreme violence and guerilla tactics. Most Appalachian bushwhackers were pro-Confederacy. Although some of their destructive violence was levied against the population centers of the region, most of the bushwhackers' Appalachian victims were from the countryside. John Singleton Mosby was a pro-Confederate bushwhacker who raided the Union forces during the Shenandoah Campaign. His forces became a thorn in the side of the Union and bitterness between Mosby's forces and the northern troops escalated as both sides executed their helpless prisoners. Mosby's elusiveness and his ability to avoid capture led to him being awarded the soubriquet the "Gray Ghost." Despite being seriously injured on several occasions, Mosby survived the Civil War and lived until 1916.

The notorious William Clarke Quantrill was also a pro-Confederate guerilla leader. Quantrill was a well-educated drifter who fell into defending Missouri farmers against the jayhawkers, anti-slavery guerillas. Quantrill became a hired gun, involved in cattle rustling and capturing runaway slaves, and his life degenerated into mindless violence. His 1863 raid on Lawrence, Kansas descended into a bloody massacre in which at least 185 men and boys were murdered in cold blood. The massacre was described as the "most infamous event of the uncivil war." It sparked reprisal attacks against the innocent people of Western Missouri where unarmed men and boys were killed and many

homes were torched.

Appalachian law and order effectively broke down during the Civil War years, and the area became notorious for its querulous feuding people. Its history became peppered by shootouts, gunfights, ambushes, and family feuds. This lawlessness was sometimes viewed as the inevitable result of the Appalachian lack of education and the rampant poverty of the region. This became a stereotype that many people began to attach to the area and in turn led to an Appalachian distrust of the government and any form of authority that persisted for decades.

The Appalachian Economy

From the beginning of Appalachian settlement, the terrain of the region meant that it was difficult to farm profitably and most agricultural activity was done at a subsistence level. Early

Left: Devil Anse's cousin Floyd Hatfield. Randall McCoy accused Floyd of stealing one of his hogs. Perry Cline encouraged Randall to take court action, but Floyd was acquitted due to Bill Staton's perjured testimony. Staton's subsequent murder brought the feud to boiling point.

Appalachian crops included sweet potatoes, corn, squashes, tobacco, and apples. Of course, livestock was also kept. Pigs were particularly suited to rooting on the woody slopes of the region, but cattle and sheep were also introduced by the incoming settlers and grazed the upland meadows.

Logging and timber also became an important source of employment, but the lack of good roads and railroads held the success of this industry back. It was not until the 1880s, when the more accessible woodlands of the Carolinas had been exploited, that industrial-scale logging finally came to Appalachia.

Coal mining became crucial to the economy of the region and became an iconic part of Appalachian tradition. The area contained more than two-thirds of the nation's coal reserves as the Appalachian coalfield extended to over sixty-three thousand square miles. Some people have said that the region's coal fields are the single most valuable natural asset in the world. In the post-Civil War period the demand for coal was greatly stimulated by the growth of the American railroad industry. But the cyclical nature of the coal mining industry also brought serious economic problems into the region. Coal mining was dependent on demand from other industries, such as steel fabrication, and this led to constant hiring and firing of the workforce. This in turn led to bitter labor disputes which sometimes descended into violence. The region's dependence on coal mining to provide many of its jobs also resulted in terrible mining accidents and the ill health of many of its workforce.

Like so many Appalachian families, the Hatfields and McCoys were both active in several aspects of the region's economic activity, including farming, coal mining, and logging. Their family histories very much reflected the labor profile of the region.

Right: Johnse Hatfield and Roseanna McCoy. The couple was never married and their daughter Sarah Elizabeth McCoy Hatfield survived for just eight months.

Appalachian Culture

Religious diversity is also a powerful force in Appalachia, and the region has its own spiritual customs and practices. Many of the original European settlers came to the region to avoid religious intolerance in their own countries and were often of an evangelical persuasion. Once in the region, they evolved their own special brand of Appalachian Christianity. This included some original practices including natural water or creek baptism, chanting, snake handling, and foot washing. Protestantism is the dominant religion of the region but includes many different sects including the Presbyterians, Baptists, Methodists, Pentecostals, and Mennonites.

Like its religion, Appalachian education developed slightly differently than in the rest of America's. In the nineteenth century, education in the region lagged behind the national norm. One-room schoolhouses were commonplace and it was quite usual for

Right: The most
famous Appalachian
dish is dried apple
stack cake.

children to attend them on an *ad hoc* basis when they were not required for farm work. Education was made compulsory after the Civil War but there were still many settlement schools in the rural areas of the region.

Music has always had a central position in Appalachian culture. The region's musical tradition was derived from the folk music of Scotland and Ireland. Banjos are often added to the original fiddle tunes to create an original form of country folk music and bluegrass. Dozens of music festivals are now held in the region each year. Appalachian literature has also taken its own unique forms as its isolation led to untrammeled individualism. The unique Appalachian experience has spawned many folk heroes, such as John Henry, a legendary railroad construction worker. He died in 1887 after winning an exhausting steel-driving competition with a steam-powered hammer. Davy Crockett was another example of a real-life character drawn into many Appalachian legends and stories.

One of the most popular aspects of the Appalachian tradition is its indigenous cuisine. Using the diverse produce of the region, many dishes melded the culinary tradition of the original Native American inhabitants with that of the incoming European immigrants. Signature foods of the region include chicken and dumplings, apple butter, biscuits and gravy, deviled eggs, rhubarb, green beans, country ham, kraut, grits, venison, squirrel, pheasant,

peas, pears, and baked sweet potatoes. Perhaps the most famous Appalachian dish is dried apple stack cake, often served as a wedding cake. Traditionally, each wedding guest brought a layer of cake and the layers were then sandwiched together with apple butter. Although Appalachian regional cuisine is not very sophisticated, its wholesome, natural ingredients ensure that it is delicious.

A unique marriage tradition also grew up in Appalachia. Marriages were usually arranged by senior family members. Appalachian families were usually highly patriarchal so it was fathers that organized unions between their children. Courtships were short, usually lasting just two or three weeks before the wedding, and the couple was usually very young. Brides were usually aged between thirteen and fifteen years old, and grooms were usually a couple of years older. Unarranged relationships were strongly disapproved of, but if a girl became pregnant by an unapproved suitor, a "shotgun" wedding would usually be arranged by her family.

Appalachian society was highly male-dominated and a wife was expected to defer to her husband in everything. Not only were women expected to eat in the kitchen after serving their menfolk, but a woman usually walked a few paces behind her husband when out in public. Women were encouraged to bear a child each year as this was thought to keep them faithful to their husbands. Inevitably, this led to an early death for many Appalachian women. It was

Left: The Murder of Ellison Hatfield took place at the Kentucky election grounds in April 1882. He was stabbed and shot to death by Tolbert, Pharmer, and Bud McCoy. His death was to unleash a series of murders committed by both the Hatfields and the McCoys.

therefore not uncommon for a man to marry three or four times and father as many as thirty or forty children.

Several of these marital traditions surfaced in the intertwined story of the Hatfield and McCoy families and became another of the many grievances that stoked the hostility between them.

Appalachian Blood Feuds

Blood feuds and family vendettas have been an intrinsic part of the history of the Appalachian region. These have often escalated from trivial disputes into widespread feuds and even range wars. Feuds were particularly prevalent in the lawless years around the Civil War, many a continuation of the hostilities. The feud between the Hatfield and McCoy families was perhaps the most notorious of these, but there were plenty of other infamous examples. This tendency to feud has been partly attributed to the Scottish and Irish ancestry of many of the participants. Clan warfare was rife in both of these Celtic nations and often continued for generations. Many feuds started with disputes about land, cattle, or sexual rivalry and escalated into small local wars that sometimes involved hundreds of combatants.

The Martin-Tolliver Feud

The Martin and Tolliver families both came from the Kentucky hillbilly tradition, where family disputes often resulted in violence on the state's "dark and bloody ground." Their family conflict was so severe that it also became known as the Rowan County War. It resulted in the deaths of twenty men and sixteen more were wounded. The dispute started in 1884 when John Martin accidentally wounded Floyd Tolliver. His intended victim was Tolliver's friend Solomon Bradley. Just as the wounding incident came to court, Martin finally shot and killed Floyd Tolliver in a barroom brawl. Tolliver's dying words were prophetic: "Remember what you swore to do; you said you would kill him; keep your word." The Rowan County War culminated in 1887 with a two-and-a-half-hour-long shootout between sixty combatants. It ended with the death of Sheriff Craig Tolliver on the streets of Morehead, Kentucky. The families were finally reconciled in 1899 when Grace Martin and Frank Tolliver were married.

The French-Eversole Feud

The French and Eversole families were equally combative and their enmity resulted in one of the largest-ever Kentucky feuds.

Their family war raged between 1887 and 1894 and resulted in as many as seventy deaths and many children being orphaned. Both clan leaders, Joseph C. Eversole and Benjamin Fulton French, were from Hazard, Kentucky. Atypically both were well-educated lawyers and businessmen. Although the two men were friendly, their commercial rivalry soon spiraled out of control. Silas Gayheart, a close friend of Benjamin French, was the first fatality in the feud. Another French sympathizer, Bill Gambrial, was the next victim. A series of deadly ambushes followed. Tom Smith lay in wait for Joseph Eversole and Nicholas Combs, the nephew of Judge Josiah Combs, and shot and killed both men before stealing from their corpses. Smith also murdered Dr. John R. Roder in a drunken rage.

Hazard descended into complete lawlessness and Kentucky governor Buckner ordered troops into the town. A general shootout followed with further fatalities. In the aftermath of the conflagration Judge Lily staged a series of trials in a tent courthouse. Tom Smith was hanged and several others were imprisoned. Although calm gradually returned to Hazard, a further bout of violence occurred in 1913 when Harry Eversole shot Fulton French, who died from the wound a year later.

The Hargis-Marcum-Callahan-Cockerell Feud

The Hargis-Marcum-Callahan-Cockerell feud took place in Breathitt County, Kentucky in and around the town of Jackson. The hostilities dated back to the Civil War when the area raised two regiments, one for the Confederates and one for the Union side. Although most of the county families were related to each other in one way or another, the feudists joined a conflict that claimed many lives. Ironically several of the combatants were employed in various forms of law enforcement.

The conflict began in 1899 over charges of electoral fraud and in 1902 town marshal Tom Cockerell shot and killed Ben Hargis in the Blind Tiger Saloon. James B. Marcum was murdered in 1903 and Breathitt County descended into a vortex of murder plots, assassinations, assaults, shootings, drownings, and axe attacks. With the murder of town marshal Jim Cockerell, Jackson descended into lawlessness. County sheriff Ed Callahan was too afraid to discharge his duties and the town slid into anarchy. Over thirty people were murdered in the course of the feud including two women, Susan Barnett and Mrs. Luneford, but no one was ever convicted of their murders. The hostilities rumbled on until the patriarchs of the Hargis and Callahan families were killed in 1908 and 1912.

The White-Garrard Feud

The White-Garrard feud was unusual in that the protagonists were highly educated Appalachian business oligarchs. Both families were from Manchester in Clay County, Kentucky and had made their fortunes from the salt industry there. Manchester's salt works had made the town strategically important during the Civil War and it was held by both Union and Confederate troops. Men from the town also served on both sides of the conflict. The families also had different political allegiances. The Whites were Whigs, while the Garrards were Democrats. The rivalry between the two families ensured that the town became a breeding ground for feuding violence. Because the families were wealthy and prominent, they drew many other local people into their quarrel. The first killing of the feud happened in 1865 when Ed White shot John Bowling, the Garrard candidate for county jailer. The hostilities rumbled on, sometimes on the streets and sometimes in court. In 1898 the state militia was called to police the trial of Tom Baker, part of the Garrard faction. Even while the militia was in the town, Baker was killed on the courtroom steps by a sniper shooting from the home of Sheriff Bev White.

The feud raged on for decades and continued to reverberate until 1932. It had a seriously detrimental effect on the reputation of Clay County, which was seen as a hotbed of violence and ignorance.

Right: Craig Tolliver was shot to death on the streets of Morehead, Rowan County, on June 22, 1887. He died with his brothers, Jay and Budd. When he died Craig was the leader of the Tolliver gang.

Devil Anse Hatfield's Colt Bisley Revolver

Anse Hatfield's Colt Bisley revolver

Famous sharpshooter Devil Anse Hatfield owned a Colt Bisley
Model revolver. The name of this celebrated weapon is derived
from England's famous Bisley firing range. The Bisley was a special
target version of the popular Colt Single Action Army Model
and was marketed between 1894 and 1915. The Bisley shared the
same cylinder, barrel, and ejector rod with the Single Action. The
gun can be distinguished from the ordinary Colt Single Action
by the half-moon shape missing from the top of the larger grip,
the wider hammer spur, and the wider trigger. On this model, the
top strap is flat and machined to take an adjustable sight. The front
sight is a removable blade that slots into the top of the barrel. It
is interchangeable with different blades to adjust to the sighting
elevation.

The Bisley was introduced as a target pistol, but it is highly unlikely that Devil Anse bought the gun for firing on the shooting range. Most guns sold in the American market were bought for self-defense and the Bisley was no exception to this. The Bisley's larger grip and wider hammer made it perfect for quick shooting.

The serial numbers used for the Bisley were sequential to those of the Colt Peacemaker. The Bisley was equipped with a plain barrel up to number 161376, but later versions had "Bisley Model" stamped on the barrel. Devils Anse's Bisley has a plain barrel which means it is one of the earlier guns from the 1890s. The Bisley was offered in several different Colt calibers: 32-20, 38-40, .45 Colt, 44-40, and .41 Colt. Over forty-four thousand Bisleys were manufactured.

Left: A beautiful young Roseanna McCoy. Roseanna was the ninth child of Randall and Sarah McCoy. She was one of six McCoy children to die as a result of the feud.

THE FEUD BEGINS: THE CIVIL WAR YEARS

The Civil War was ignited by the issue of slavery, but with the secession of the pro-slavery Southern states, the war soon became about the preservation of the Union itself. As President Lincoln said, "A house divided against itself cannot stand. I believe that government cannot endure permanently half slave and half free." With his election, control of the nation's government passed to the North for the first time in several generations, and hostilities seemed inevitable. When it came, the conflict touched almost every American family in some way or another, and there was no escape for either the Hatfields or the McCoys. Both families served in the conflict and were damaged by it.

The Appalachian region was particularly badly hit by the conflict. The people of the mountain states were bitterly divided by the issue of slavery. The northern part of the region was mostly pro-abolitionist, while most southern Appalachians wanted to retain the *status quo*. This resulted in a miniature version of the Civil War that preceded the events of the nationwide conflict

Right: The entrance to the Hatfield family cemetery.

66

Left: Sarah McCoy begged Devil Anse Hatfield to spare her three sons' lives. Her intercession was fruitless and the boys died in a hail of bullets.

by several years. Some of the bitterest fighting of the War itself was between the so-called jayhawkers and bushwhackers in the mountain region. The vicious and barbaric methods of these mountain guerillas were epitomized by such men as Bloody Bill Quantrill. The brutal Quantrill specialized in murdering innocent civilians and devastating their homes. It is said that the official battles brought less destruction to the mountain counties than the frequent raids mounted by these unofficial combatants did.

During the Civil War years, the two families lived on either side of the Tug Fork River. At the time, this was an isolated area with no road or rail communications. The Hatfields were based in Mingo County, West Virginia, while the McCoys lived in Pike County, Kentucky. These were stable and rather static communities in which the families both thrived. Although they lived in simple log dwellings, both Devil Anse and his wife Levisa and Randall McCoy and his wife Sarah each had more than a dozen children. The Hatfields and McCoys travelled backwards and forwards across the River Tug to socialize, trade, and even marry with each other. Over the decades the families became deeply entwined. The Hatfields and McCoys had been among the first families to settle the Tug Valley, but the Hatfields soon became more affluent. Devil Anse Hatfield ran a profitable lumber mill near the Tug River and employed dozens of men. Randall McCoy was also in the timber business, but the Hatfield concern was much more successful. Ironically, Devil Anse employed three McCoys in his timber business: Albert McCoy, Lorenzo Dow McCoy, and Selkirk McCoy.

The Families Take Sides

When the Civil War broke out, the Hatfields fought for the Confederacy and so did most of the McCoys. Most members of both families favored the anti-abolitionist position of the South. Devil Anse Hatfield served in the Confederate Virginia infantry for two years and gained the "Devil" soubriquet from the fierceness he showed in the fighting.

He enlisted as a private in the Confederate army in July 1862 and was quickly promoted to first lieutenant. Anse first joined the Virginia State Line unit. The purpose of this division was to protect the borders of Kentucky and South Carolina from Union insurgency. Anse and his unit fought in several battles in Mingo, Logan, and Pike counties. Hatfield subsequently joined the regular Confederate States of America Army and served in the 45th Virginia Infantry. Several McCoys also served in the 45th. But Anse soon became disillusioned with military service and deserted the regular army in February 1863. He knew that the Confederate cause was lost and felt that he should go home and take care of his own family. He subsequently organized and led a guerilla

Right: When Devil Anse Hatfield was told of his brother Ellison's death, he ordered the execution of the three McCoy brothers. Known as "Little Randall," Bud McCoy was only fifteen when he was executed.

company, an offshoot of the Logan Wildcats, which raged through the region as bushwhackers, but he took no further action in the regular army.

Devil Anse's younger brother Ellison Hatfield also fought for the Confederacy. A large, handsome, and easygoing man, Ellison was first mustered in December 1863 and joined the 45th Battalion of the Virginia Infantry, where he soon rose to the rank of first lieutenant. Later that year he took part in the ill-fated Pickett's charge of July 7, 1863. This disastrous action was ordered by General Robert E. Lee on the last day of the Battle of Gettysburg. Major General George Pickett was one of three Confederate generals who led the charge of 12,500 Confederate troops on the elevated Union position of Cemetery Ridge. From the beginning of the assault, the Confederates came under heavy Union fire from the raised ground of the ridge and thousands of men were killed or injured. The maneuver was a complete disaster and the Confederate forces suffered appalling casualties of more than fifty percent.

The Southern war effort never recovered from this futile charge which demonstrated both the inept leadership of the Confederate forces and their poor equipment. Gettysburg was a turning point in the war that effectively ended any hope of a Confederate victory. When General Lee finally surrendered at Appomattox Court House on April 9, 1865, Ellison Hatfield was one of the junior Confederate officers who surrendered with him. The shame and disappointment after three years of terrible fighting must have been crushing.

Ellison finally returned to his Appalachian home in July 1865 and married Bill Staton's sister, Sarah Ann Staton. The couple went on to have eleven children. Sadly, Ellison's Civil War sufferings were not to be the end of his miseries.

Most of the McCoys also fought for the Confederacy. The leader of the clan, Randolph, or Randall, McCoy joined the 36th Virginia Infantry in 1861. Like Devil Anse Hatfield Randolph joined up early and the paths of their military service seem to have crossed on more than one occasion. But unlike Devil Anse, Randall fought to the bitter end of the conflict.

As the war ground on, Randall was transferred to the 45th Battalion of the Virginia Infantry, which had been mustered to the Confederate cause in April 1863. McCoy gained promotion to the rank of Lieutenant Colonel in April 1863. Later that year he was involved in a successful action against Union General Bill France's Third Corps. Legend has it that Devil Anse was also involved in this action and that he and McCoy subsequently became marked men. Randall was taken prisoner by the Union forces and held in captivity from July 1863 to June 1865. He was originally kept prisoner at Camp Chase, Ohio before being transferred to Kemper Barracks, Ohio. Finally Randall was moved to the notorious Camp Douglas in Chicago, Illinois. Camp Douglas was infamous for the terrible treatment that was meted out to Confederate prisoners of war there. The camp conditions were so bad that many prisoners died of smallpox or typhoid; others starved or simply froze to death in the terrible conditions. The camp was filthy and vermin-ridden and it was said that vegetables were deliberately withheld from the inmates so that they fell sick with scurvy. The camp guards ran a cruel and violent regime against the helpless inmates. As many as one in four prisoners died at the camp and in the final indignity, many of their bodies were sold to medical schools. Unsurprisingly, there were many attempts to escape from the camp, including the famous Camp Douglas Conspiracy of 1864.

Randall survived his wartime incarceration and was released in June 1865 in return for taking the oath of allegiance to the Union. It is said that he despised Devil Anse for his early desertion of the Confederate cause. Always known as a serious and humorless man, Randall's terrible sufferings may well have embittered him against the Hatfield patriarch. He returned home to find his wife Sarah and their children all but starving while the deserter Devil Anse Hatfield had used the intervening years to build up his timber business.

The notorious exception to this general loyalty to the Confederacy was Asa Harmon McCoy, Randall's brother, who

Right: A dramatic line-drawing of the execution of the three McCoy brothers. The sketch illustrated a *New York World* newspaper article by Theron C. Crawford. Crawford wrote a series of articles about the feud that was published between 1882 and 1890. In 1888, some of Crawford's articles were collected and published as a book entitled *An American Vendetta; a Story of Barbarism in the United States.*

EXECUTION OF THE
THREE M'COY BOYS.

fought for the Union side. As the clan patriarch's brother, Asa was a senior member of the McCoy family and his military service for the Union resulted in bad blood between these two mountain families. Asa enlisted as a Union army private in 1861, using the slightly disguised name of Asa. H. McCay. Maybe he was aware that his army service would make him a social pariah.

The division of the McCoy family loyalties reflected the state of Kentucky itself. Originally Kentucky had been neutral, but after the Confederacy failed to take the state, it fell under solid Union control. Kentucky was one of those states in which the fighting of the Civil War really meant "brother against brother," which was reflected in the McCoy family's war service. Ironically, Kentucky was the birthplace of both Union President Abraham Lincoln and Confederate President Jefferson Davis.

Asa served in the Union army for just a few months before he was wounded in February or March of 1862. He was shot near the collarbone and the bullet travelled right through his body. He was taken home to recover or die. As he lay near death, Asa was captured by the Confederate Virginia Cavalry and taken prisoner. Around a year later, he was exchanged for a Confederate prisoner. Poor Asa had had no proper medical attention during his captivity as his year-old wound was still infected and he was almost prostrate from the effects of the injury. Once more McCoy was taken home to recuperate. By October 1863 he was well enough to re-enlist and joined the 45th Regiment of the Kentucky Volunteer Mounted Infantry. This troop had been mustered by Colonel John Mason Brown in October 1863. (The regiment was disbanded at the end of the conflict in 1865.) Asa fought for the Union for just over a year before being wounded for a second time. This time, his leg was broken. He was discharged from military service on Christmas Eve 1864. For a third and last time, Asa returned to the Tug Valley to recover from his wounds. But this time his welcome home was more equivocal. He had been warned off coming back into the area by Jim Vance, Devil Anse's uncle, but he came home all the same. Back in the Tug Valley, and still wearing his Union jacket, Asa very unwisely boasted of serving "Old Abe" and asserted that the South would soon be rejoining the Union. Infuriated, Vance and Hatfield decided to take care of this traitor to the southern cause.

As the injured man hid out at home, he was attacked with a hail of bullets as he drew water from the well. Fearful for his life, Asa fled his family cabin and hid in a nearby cave at Blue Spring Creek where his loyal ex-slave Pete secretly brought him food and drink. Even poor white Appalachians were often slave owners while many black Appalachians welcomed the Union forces that swept through the region and left with them as they moved on. Unfortunately, Devil Anse's Wildcats tracked Pete's footprints through the snow and discovered McCoy's hideout.

Left: Devil Anse, Ellison, and Smith Hatfield. Smith Hatfield survived both of his brothers and died in 1937.

Run to ground, Asa Harmon McCoy was shot and murdered by an unidentified gunman on January 7, 1865, just four months before the end of the Civil War. His lifeless body was discovered by his widow, Martha Patty Cline McCoy, slumped over a snow-covered log. Devil Anse Hatfield was the original suspect for the killing, but it turned out that he was at home in bed during the shooting. The gunman is now thought to have been Wheeler Wilson, acting on Jim Vance's orders.

Ironically, even the McCoy clan felt that Asa had brought his fate upon himself by siding with the Union cause. The case drifted and no one was ever tried for the cold-blooded killing of a wounded man.

It is worth looking at the death in context. Law enforcement and the government itself seemed very distant to the Appalachian people, who tended to rely on their own family units for protection. Family patriarchs like Devil Anse Hatfield and Randall McCoy dispensed justice without reference to any outside agencies. Although the people of the region were intelligent and resourceful, many were illiterate, increasing their sense of isolation. Asa Harmon McCoy's maverick actions seemed to fly in the face of the accepted way of life in the Tug Valley and he paid a heavy price for them.

Many people count Asa Harmon McCoy as the first casualty of the bloody feud between the Hatfields and the McCoys. He wasn't destined to be the last. His death undoubtedly caused the desire for revenge to simmer in the hearts of the McCoys and may well have lit the long fuse that was to cause the friction between the two families to explode into further violence.

Both the Hatfields and the McCoys suffered dreadfully during the Civil War; the horrors of the conflict may well have intensified the bitterness of the feud itself. The terrible experiences that men from both families had endured hardened and acclimatized them to violence and suffering. Many modern students of the feud believe that several of its participants, including Devil Anse Hatfield and Randall McCoy, were probably suffering from post-traumatic stress disorder.

The Timber Dispute

The families were now on a collision course. Their bad feelings surfaced in a relatively trivial court case in the late 1870s when the Hatfields and McCoys found themselves on opposing sides.

Perry A. Cline was a wealthy land owner, having jointly inherited five thousand acres from his father, the so-called "Rich" Jake Cline who had been a prosperous landowner in the Tug River Valley. Perry's brother Jacob Cline Jr. was the co-owner of the property. Perry Cline was a member of the extended McCoy clan. He had married Martha Adkins in 1868 but his sister Martha

Left: Nancy McCoy was the daughter of Asa Harmon McCoy and Martha Patty Cline McCoy. She was born in Pike County, Kentucky in 1860 and died there in 1901.

Cline was married to Asa Harmon McCoy, the brother of clan patriarch Randall McCoy. Cline's misfortune was that his land holding was located in Logan County, West Virginia, adjacent to Devil Anse Hatfield's property. In 1872 Devil Anse brought a court action against Cline, accusing him of cutting timber on Hatfield land. In 1877, Anse won the case and was awarded Cline's five thousand acres as compensation for the loss of his timber. It was widely believed that the Hatfields' political influence had delivered the verdict to Devil Anse, together with Cline's valuable property.

The defeated Cline relocated to Pike County, Kentucky. He went on to become a prosperous lawyer, a deputy sheriff, and a deputy jailer. Cline also formed a close relationship with Randall McCoy. Embittered by the loss of his property, Cline used his powerful position to pursue revenge against the Hatfields. Later in the feud, he attempted to bring them to Kentucky to be tried for the murder of Bill Staton. Cline also campaigned for Kentucky governor Simon Bolivar Buckner who had promised to bring the Hatfields to justice. Buckner himself genuinely believed that the Hatfield hillbillies were damaging the economic prospects of the Appalachian region. In a direct reference to the feuding family's murder of Bill Staton, Buckner asserted, "If we fail to repress this lawlessness, or bring the offenders to justice, we have no right to complain of the false estimation in which we are held by the people of other states."

This ill feeling served to keep the feud at simmering point.

The Hog Trouble

Hostilities between the two families burst into actual violence just a year later in 1878, when Floyd Hatfield and Randall McCoy fell into a violent dispute over the ownership of a hog. This is not as trivial as it sounds. Hog farming was extremely important to the Appalachian economy in the mid-nineteenth century. In 1860, the region's farm animals were worth twice as much as its cotton crop. Pigs were the most plentiful livestock in Appalachia next to sheep. Appalachian farmers produced two-thirds of America's hogs, which were worth an astounding one hundred million dollars each year. Wealthy planters often contracted with poor local farmers to sharecrop pigs on their mountainous farmland. The planters supplied the livestock, equipment, and, before the Civil War, specially trained slaves to look after the pigs. It is estimated that around ten percent of adult male slaves were employed in this way. Poor Appalachian farmers oversaw the pig-rearing for a share of the livestock. They often burnt over the mountain balds to increase their pastureland. Young pigs were usually raised in the wild, roving in the woods to eat acorns and chestnuts. They were also let loose near the farmhouses and slave quarters to dispose of any food scraps and garbage. Twice a year, litters of piglets were born in the woods and earmarked by their owners with a series of distinctive notches. The pigs were trained to come to a whistle and about a month before they were due for slaughter they were penned and fed on corn, since their diet of acorns and chestnuts made their meat and lard taste bitter. Pork meat was sold all over the region and to company towns at the nearby copper mines. Meat processing became one of the most important businesses in Appalachia. Pork meat was salted, smoked, and barreled. A great quantity of preserved meat was then exported to the Northern states. Pork was also exported on the hoof. Highly skilled drovers brought fattened animals to market in massive livestock drives. Over one million pigs a year were exported from the region in this extremely profitable trade.

As the primary source of meat in Appalachia, pork was celebrated in many of the region's iconic dishes. These include Smithfield ham, bacon, preserved pork, pork chops, hog maws, chitterlings, sausages, trotters, sausage gravy, ham hocks, and hog head cheese.

The hog trouble happened in the fall of 1878. Randall McCoy paid a visit to his wife's brother-in-law Floyd Hatfield at his Blackberry Creek farm. While he was there he spotted a hog that was earmarked with his distinctive pattern of notches. Floyd Hatfield, who happened to be a cousin of Devil Anse Hatfield,

vigorously maintained that the pig was his and that the notches on the animal's ears were those used to identify his livestock. Randall McCoy was incensed by this assertion and decided to instigate court proceedings to prove that the animal had been stolen. It was said that Perry Cline encouraged McCoy to take legal action. Ironically, Floyd Hatfield lived on the Kentucky side of the River Tug so the legal action took place in McCoy territory. Despite this the local magistrate who presided over the court was none other than Reverend Anderson "Preacher Anse" Hatfield, also a close connection of Devil Anse. In a show of doing the right thing, Preacher Anse assembled an evenly split jury to try the case that was made up of six Hatfields and six McCoys. But one of the McCoy jurors, Selkirk McCoy, the nephew of Sarah McCoy, was having an affair with a Hatfield woman and voted in favor of Floyd Hatfield. Bill Staton was the star witness for the Hatfield camp and testified that the hog belonged to Floyd. Although Staton was the nephew of Randolph McCoy, he was married to a Hatfield woman and testified on behalf of his brother-in-law Floyd Hatfield. Staton testified that he had seen Floyd Hatfield notch the pig's ears proving that the animal was his.

The jury awarded victory and the pig to Floyd Hatfield but the success of the trial made his friend Bill Staton a sitting target for McCoy revenge. It also left the McCoys feeling betrayed by the justice system and more inclined to take the law into

Left: Kentucky lawman Frank Phillips murdered Hatfield clan member Jim Vance. He himself was shot to death in 1898 at the age of thirty-six.

their own hands.

Retribution came within two years of the trial. In June 1880, Randall's nephews Paris and Sam McCoy shot Bill Staton to death while he was out hunting. Sam McCoy stood trial for the murder in September 1880. Devil Anse's uncle Valentine "Wall" Hatfield was the trial judge. The prosecutor was yet another Hatfield brother, Ellison Hatfield, who also happened to be Bill Staton's brother-in-law. He raised warrants to bring Paris and Sam to trial.

Despite the complete Hatfield control of the trial, Sam McCoy maintained that he had killed Staton in self-defense and was acquitted. It was said that Devil Anse Hatfield was instrumental in the court finding in favor of the defendants. He had tried to spare Sam and Paris McCoy from being tried for the murder at all. He wanted to keep relations between the families as calm as possible. But this was a hopeless aspiration, and doomed to failure.

The Romeo and Juliet of the Hills

The next bloody collision between the two families resulted from the doomed love story of Johnse (Johnson) Hatfield and Roseanna McCoy. Johnse was Devil Anse Hatfield's eldest son and Roseanna was Randall McCoy's daughter. Although he was still in his teens, Johnse had a reputation for being a notorious womanizer. Roseanna's reputation is harder to pin down. She is

Left: Jim Vance bludgeoned Sarah McCoy with a rifle butt as the McCoy homestead burned. This drawing first appeared in the *New York World* newspaper in the 1880s. It illustrated an article by Theron C. Crawford. Crawford interviewed Devil Anse Hatfield and described the patriarch as a "jovial old pirate."

alternatively described as a pure and sheltered mountain girl or a sexually experienced woman riddled with gonorrhea. Either way Roseanna was a beautiful woman who became completely smitten with Johnse when they first met at the Kentucky election grounds in 1880. The couple came together almost immediately. Johnse promised Roseanna love and marriage and she moved into the Hatfield homestead. The inevitable soon happened, and Roseanna fell pregnant. Roseanna assumed that Johnse would marry her in one of the shotgun weddings that were so common in the Appalachians. But despite the pregnancy, neither the Hatfields nor the McCoys would give the couple their blessing to get married. Although he was estranged from his daughter, Randolph McCoy felt that a shotgun wedding to a Hatfield would ruin her. Strangely, the Hatfields' objections were more practical. They knew that Johnse had been unfaithful to Roseanna throughout their relationship. Devil Anse was disgusted by his son's behavior and Johnse's mother Levisa (Levicy) Chafin Hatfield was convinced that the marriage would be doomed from the start and asked Roseanna to leave the Hatfield home. Levisa was a typical Appalachian matriarch whose word was law in the family home. Ironically it is likely that the couple were already legally married. Both West Virginia and Kentucky were Common Law States where a couple can marry by simply stating their mutual consent to the union. No formal ceremony or religious service was necessary.

Although Roseanna was estranged from her family, her brothers were outraged by the degrading treatment she had received at the hands of the Hatfields. They felt that her shame would not be expunged until Johnse had been punished or killed. The McCoy boys, including special deputy Tolbert McCoy, surprised the two lovers one evening and captured Johnse. They claimed that they were enforcing Kentucky warrants that had been issued for Johnse's arrest and would take him to Pikeville jail. Roseanna knew that they would kill her lover unless she intervened. Borrowing a neighbor's horse, the frantic young woman rode bareback to tell Devil Anse Hatfield of Johnse's abduction. This became known as her infamous "midnight ride." Anse immediately got a posse together and rode after his son, reclaiming him without a scratch. But he refused to punish the McCoy brothers as he felt that Johnse had brought their anger on himself with his loose sexual behavior.

Roseanna herself was the biggest loser. Despite her unwavering loyalty to Johnse and her willingness to betray her own brothers, her lover deserted her. The pregnant Roseanna moved out of the Hatfield home.

Although Roseanna's mother Sarah McCoy wanted her daughter home, Randall refused to allow her back into the family. Roseanna moved in with her aunt Betty McCoy who

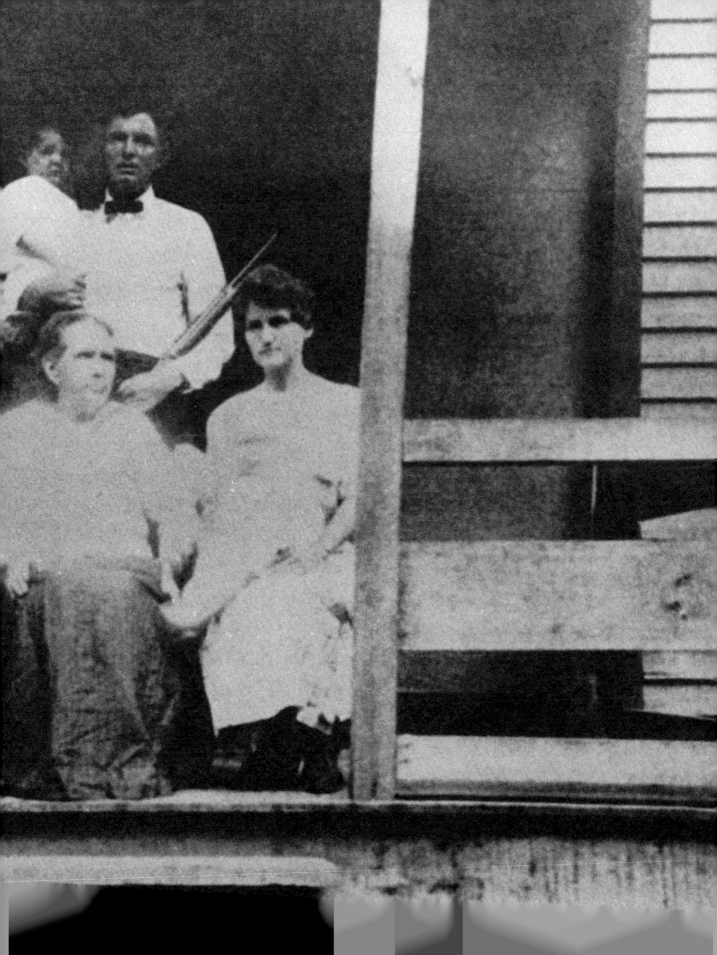

Previous pages: Devil
Anse and Levisa
Hatfield with several
other Hatfield family
members on the
Hatfield homestead
porch. Taylor Hatfield
(left) and Willis
Hatfield (right) carry
rifles to reflect the
feuding history of the
family. It is a typical
Hatfield pose.

lived at Stringtown, Kentucky. There she gave birth to her daughter Sarah Elizabeth McCoy Hatfield, named for her mother and her aunt. But the child died from measles just eight months later. The distraught Roseanna buried the child near her aunt's house, still un-reconciled with her family. In 1882 Roseanna moved into the home of the Hatfield-hating Perry Cline as the governess to his children.

Johnse Hatfield married Roseanna's cousin, twenty-year-old Nancy McCoy, on May 14, 1881. Nancy was born in 1860 in Pike County, Kentucky. She was the daughter of Asa Harmon McCoy – the same Asa Harmon who had been gunned down on Devil Anse Hatfield's instructions when she was just five years old – and Perry Cline's sister Martha Cline McCoy. Although Johnse and Nancy had two children, the marriage was a disaster and did absolutely nothing to heal the rift between the two families. Johnse's subsequent life went from bad to worse. Nancy left him and moved back to the McCoy's home state of Kentucky. Her total rejection of Johnse culminated in her re-marriage to his pursuer, the bounty hunter and sometime Kentucky lawman Bad Frank Phillips. Nancy had finally had her revenge against the Hatfields for her father's murder.

After the next bout of feuding it was Nancy's second husband who finally brought the Hatfields to justice. He was also responsible for the shooting of Devil Anse Hatfield's uncle Jim

Vance. Phillips boasted that he would be the family's nemesis. Womanizing Johnse Hatfield went on to re-marry three more times and had two more children, one of whom died in early infancy. He survived until 1822 and died at the age of eighty.

But Roseanna's devastation and the death of her young daughter did not end the tragic repercussions of this poisonous relationship. She died of a broken heart at the age of twenty-eight. Although she had never been fully re-integrated into the McCoy family, they believed that the Hatfields were responsible for her death.

The Death of Ellison Hatfield

The McCoys finally took their revenge for Nancy's shame at the 1882 Election Day gathering. This was held at Jerry Hatfield's farm where the locals gathered to vote for local officials and set school taxes. This lively social event, complete with music and dancing, had been the scene of Johnse and Roseanna's first meeting just two years before.

The Hatfields and McCoys were both in attendance and the atmosphere of the gathering was highly charged for both families. The McCoys felt insulted by the Hatfields' treatment of Roseanna and by Johnse's escape from their attempted retribution. A quarrel between the families was almost inevitable, but no one could have

Previous spread:
Four members of the
extended Hatfield
clan enjoy a hunting
expedition. Left to
right, they are Ock
Damron, Devil Anse
Hatfield, Jim Vance,
and W.B. Borden.
Jim Vance was Devil
Anse's uncle.

seen the devastating consequences that ensued.

Ellison Hatfield was a large and affable man and the father of thirteen children. He was also Devil Anse's elder brother and accompanied him to the Election Day gathering. Ellison arrived wearing a large straw hat. The McCoys taunted him about his eccentric headgear, but Ellison laughed it off. The squabble between the two camps escalated as the McCoys tried to make Bad Lias Hatfield hand over a small amount of money that he owed them for a fiddle. The general ill feeling led to a verbal fight between Tolbert McCoy and Ellison, during which Ellison was supposed to have referred to Tolbert as a "damn hog." The quarrel then descended into a general brawl between Ellison and three of Randolph McCoy's sons, Roseanne's younger brothers: Tolbert, Pharmer, and Randolph Jr. Bud McCoy. Tolbert drew a knife and stabbed Ellison, who tried to defend himself with a rock. Before the participants were dragged apart, Ellison had been stabbed at least twenty-six times and shot in the back. The McCoy brothers fled the scene in panic.

As poor Ellison lay dying, the local law moved in and arrested the McCoy trio but a Hatfield posse of around thirty men led by Devil Anse snatched them from the law. The Hatfields forced the McCoy brothers into a skiff and took them down the Tug River back into West Virginia where they incarcerated them in an empty schoolhouse on Mate Creek. The boys' mother Sarah McCoy and her daughter-in-law Mary Butcher, Tolbert's wife, came to beg Anse to release the boys to the law. Anse refused to decide their fate until he knew if his brother would survive. He promised that if Ellison survived he would return them to Kentucky to face justice. But Anse's brother Wall Hatfield told Sarah that if Ellison died he would shoot her sons as full of holes as a sifter bottom.

Ellison had been wounded on April 7 but he lay writhing in agony until April 9 when he finally died.

The Death of the McCoy Brothers

As the news of his death reached Devil Anse, the Hatfield posse took the McCoy boys back into Kentucky and tied them to some pawpaw bushes. Devil Anse advised them to make their peace with God, and then he and the other men started shooting. Devil Anse had kept his word. Pharmer and Tolbert died in a hail of bullets and their bodies were said to be riddled with over fifty shells. Legend has it that Devil Anse considered sparing the younger brother, Bud McCoy, leaving him tied to his brothers' bodies. But as the Hatfields started for home, Devil Anse changed his mind, saying "Boys, dead men tell no tales." He dismounted and shot the fifteen-year-old Bud in the head.

The McCoy family was too scared to remove the bodies and the murdered boys remained tied to the bushes for hours. The three brothers were ultimately buried in one large coffin on the McCoy property located at the Blackberry Fork of the Pond Creek in Pike County, Kentucky.

Judge George Brown of the Pike County, Kentucky circuit court immediately assembled a grand jury to indict the Hatfields for this premeditated triple murder. Twenty men were charged with involvement in the crime, including Devil Anse Hatfield, two of his brothers, his sons Johnse and Cap, and family friend Selkirk McCoy, who had swung the jury at the hog trial.

But the Hatfields were determined to avoid justice and became extremely security conscious. Fully aware that the rewards offered for their capture made them the target of every local bounty hunter, Anse collected a veritable armory. The Hatfields moved around in well-armed bands and the whole family retreated into a fortified stockade. This excluded Johnse Hatfield. Anse finally rejected his eldest son when it became clear that Johnse's wife Nancy had been passing on information that she had gleaned from Johnse about the Hatfields to her birth family. Devil Anse believed that Nancy's treachery had contributed to Ellison's death and was furious with Johnse. He was so angry that he is reputed to have taken his eldest son on a fishing trip with the intention of killing him in the wild. But Anse couldn't bring himself to kill his own flesh and blood and simply told his eldest son to leave the family home and find his fortune elsewhere.

Right: Valentine or Uncle Wall Hatfield was Devil Anse Hatfield's elder and less violent brother. He was one of the eight members of the Hatfield clan to be condemned for the New Year's Massacre, although it is unlikely that he took any active part in the feuding violence. Wall Hatfield died in jail in Pikeville, Kentucky waiting for his brothers to rescue him. He was buried in the prison cemetery.

Johnse was to become involved in the most unforgiveable violence of the feud and was forced into hiding. Returning to the region ten years later, he was immediately arrested, convicted, and given a life sentence. Luckily for him, he was pardoned when he saved the life of the Lieutenant Governor of Kentucky when another inmate attacked him with a knife during a prison visit.

Anse believed that it was Nancy McCoy's sister Mary McCoy Daniels who had leaked the Hatfield plans to the McCoy boys and decided to punish her for her talkative ways. In 1886 a Hatfield posse broke into her house and Cap Hatfield and Tom Wallace severely beat both Mary and her daughter with a cow's tail. Mary's brother Jeff McCoy swore revenge against Cap and Tom Wallace for the ignominious beating. But later that year, Jeff got into a brawl with Pike County mail carrier Fred Wolford at a local dance and killed him. This gave Logan County special constable Cap Hatfield the perfect excuse to track Jeff to his hideout at his sister Nancy's house. The story goes that Cap Hatfield captured Jeff and was taking him back to Pike County when McCoy broke free. Jeff ran into the River Tug, trying to make it back to McCoy territory, but sharpshooter Cap felled him with a single bullet and dumped his lifeless body in the flowing water.

This was yet another death that stoked the feud. The following year Tom Wallace was found dead and it was widely assumed that

Left: Devil Anse's son Cap Hatfield owned Chilton's Store in Hanover, West Virginia. Although he was blind in one eye, Cap was a well-known marksman. He renounced feuding violence and became a Logan County sheriff. Cap was highly intelligent and in middle age studied law by correspondence and was admitted to the bar. He died in 1930.

Previous pages:
The Hatfields'
clapboard mansion
photographed around
1900. This substantial
home was a world
away from the
family's original log
cabin home.

his death was the McCoys' revenge for Jeff.

Despite the Hatfields' widely acknowledged guilt, things gradually quieted down. Although the grief-stricken Randall McCoy desperately tried to get the Kentucky authorities to take the murderous Hatfields into custody, no one was brave enough to even attempt this. But the Hatfields themselves became even more introverted and clannish. They boiled with resentment against the McCoys as they felt that their actions in killing the McCoy boys had been entirely justified and motivated by natural vengeance.

Perry Cline's Revenge

The feud may have stayed at this simmering point for years except for the malicious intervention of Perry Cline. Still harboring a grudge for the land he had been forced to hand over to Devil Anse, Cline was now a successful attorney in Pikeville and had connections in high places. Cline was also the uncle of the beaten Mary McCoy Daniels and the murdered Jeff McCoy. He argued that the Hatfields' hillbilly violence was giving the Appalachian region a bad name and delaying the extension of the railroad into the region. This in turn was hindering the development of its coal and timber industries. This was a powerful argument and may well have been true. Cline certainly convinced his close connection Kentucky governor Simon Bolivar Buckner that the Hatfields and their ilk were standing in the way of progress. He also promised to deliver the McCoy vote to Buckner if he would round up the Hatfield murderers. Buckner announced rewards for the capture of several Hatfields, including Devil Anse, and tried to persuade the governor of West Virginia E. Willis Wilson to allow bounty hunters to pursue them into his state. Although Wilson refused, Cline convened a posse of bounty hunters including the notorious Pike County Deputy Sheriff Franklin "Bad Frank" Phillips to track down the Hatfields. Philips was a notoriously heavy drinker and violent man who married his quarry Johnse Hatfield's ex-wife Nancy McCoy Hatfield in 1895.

Cline fully understood the value of publicity and fed the story of the maverick Hatfield hillbillies to the press. Story-hungry reporters began to flood into the Tug Valley, attracted by the violence and drama of the ongoing feud, and the story of the murdering renegades went national.

One way and another, the pressure on the fugitive Hatfields was building to an intolerable level as a five hundred dollar reward was posted for the capture of Devil Anse. Hunted down and feeling cornered the Hatfield clan began to lose their grip on reality. The final and most terrible wave of monstrous violence was about to become reality.

The New Year's Massacre

The beleaguered Hatfields persuaded themselves that if they destroyed the head of the McCoy clan, they would be safe. They also wanted to make sure that there was no one to testify in any trial for the murder of the three McCoy boys.

As it was reported in West Virginia's *Daily State Journal* of February 1, 1888, "the crowning piece of deviltry was reserved for the night of January 1, 1888."

On New Year's Day, Devil Anse's son Cap and his uncle Jim Vance led a Hatfield posse of thirteen men to the McCoy hewn-log homestead located at the mouth of the Pond Creek. Although he was blind in one eye, Cap was an excellent marksman. Jim Vance was an equally violent man described by his own family as being as "mean as a damn snake." The gang also included Ellison "Cotton Top" Mounts who was the illegitimate and learning-disabled son of the late Ellison Hatfield.

The McCoy cabin was home to Randall, his wife Sarah, and his thirteen children. The Hatfield gang set fire to the wooden home as the family slept, trying to drive Randall out into the open. As their quarry fled into the freezing woods with most of the children, who were still dressed in their night clothes, the Hatfields opened fire on the fleeing family. Randall's son Calvin and his daughter Alifair were caught in a hail of gunfire and

Right: Hatfield family members on the homestead porch. Anse and Levisa are joined by their granddaughter Ossie Browning, Rossie Browning, and family friend William Dyke Garrett. "Uncle Dyke" Garrett fought with Devil Anse in the Logan Wildcats. He later became Logan County's most famous preacher and was also a celebrated fiddler. In October 1911, Dyke baptized Devil Anse in Main Island Creek.

killed. The Hatfields also caught Randall's wife Sarah as she fled from the inferno and beat her over the head with a rifle butt until they believed she was dead.

The McCoy cabin was burned to the ground and the homeless and grieving family was forced to seek refuge in the Pike County courthouse. Sarah McCoy was devastated by her grief and her terrible injuries and lay near death for several days while the distraught Randall sat at her side. She never recovered from this terrible experience and was ultimately committed to an asylum at Lexington, Kentucky. She died there some years later. Randall McCoy buried Alifair and Calvin on the family property next to their brothers Tolbert, Pharmer, and Bud.

The *Daily State Journal* quoted a deeply shocked Randall McCoy as saying, "I used to be on very friendly terms with the Hatfields before and after the war. We never had any trouble till six years ago." Randall is clearly dating the feud back to the murder of Ellison Hatfield. Randall McCoy completely avoided taking any part in the feud from this point on. He moved twenty-five miles to Pikeville, Kentucky to get away from the Hatfields and lived at a house on Main Street. Randall spent his later life operating a ferry across the Chloe Branch of the Big Sandy River. He survived in relative obscurity until 1914 when he died of injuries sustained from a cooking fire at his nephew's house.

Despite his hatred of the McCoys, it is most unlikely that Devil

Left: Preacher Uncle Dyke Garrett and Mrs. Willis Hatfield. Preacher Garrett was born in 1841 and survived until 1938.

Left: A group of
Hatfield supporters
including Cap Hatfield
gather outside the
cave that Devil Anse
used to hide in
after the New Year's
Massacre. The cave is
located just outside
Sarah Ann in Logan
County, West Virginia.

Anse himself had anything to do with the homestead massacre. Anse wanted to kill Randolph as he believed that this would end the feud by destroying the chief witness against the Hatfields, but it is highly unlikely that he would have authorized an attack on women and children. Anse was probably sickened by the cold-blooded murder of two children and the appalling attack on Sarah McCoy. He must also have realized that the Hatfield family would be punished for the atrocious massacre.

The Hatfields Pay the Price

Devil Anse was absolutely right. The violence of the botched attack appalled even the citizens of the brutalized Tug Valley. The McCoy family murders became a national scandal and the governors of both Kentucky and West Virginia were called on to bring the feuding factions under control. A law enforcement posse of around thirty men was assembled under the leadership of Deputy Sheriff Bad Frank Phillips and was said to include Randall's uncle Jim McCoy. On the night of January 6, 1888, these men crossed the Tug near Pond Creek and made their way to Jim Vance's homestead. A shootout followed and Bad Frank Phillips blasted Jim Vance to death. Legend has it that he shot an extra round into the dead man's head, to make absolutely sure he was gone. On January 9, the posse captured several members of the murderous Hatfield gang, including Wall Hatfield, three Mayhorn brothers, Tom Chambers, Rew Yancey, Selkirk McCoy, and Moses Christian. A simultaneous swoop in McDowell County, West Virginia rounded up several more gang members. The captured men were dragged across the state line back into Kentucky and incarcerated in the Pikeville county jail.

Unfortunately, this crossing of the state line resulted in a legal challenge to the validity of the men's arrest. Phillips's Kentucky posse was accused of illegally crossing the state line into West Virginia and kidnapping the Hatfield gang members. West Virginia law enforcers confronted Phillips's men at Grapevine Creek, West Virginia, near Matewan, and there was an intense shootout. Hatfield gang member Bill Dempsey was killed and another man was wounded. The feud had now escalated to such a level that the law officers of two states had become involved. The local lawmen on both sides of the river had also deputized a number of bounty-hunting "detectives" in their efforts to round up the feuding family members.

The Hatfields themselves then decided to try a litigious route out of their difficulties and filed the Mahon v. Justice Action of 1888. The case centered on Wall Hatfield's son-in-law Plyant Mahon. He and the rest of the Hatfields were protesting against what they saw as their illegal capture.

The two state governors Buckner and Wilson decided that

Right: Devil Anse's son Cap Hatfield and his stepson Joseph Glenn. Glenn's father died before he was born and Cap was an affectionate stepfather, referring to him as "my boy." The pair committed a triple murder at Matewan, West Virginia in 1896.

enough was enough and asked the United States district court in Louisville, Kentucky to determine if the Hatfield gang could be tried in Kentucky. In the interim, the defendants were taken to Louisville to hear the outcome of the case. The case was subsequently referred to the United States Supreme Court and became a national cause célèbre. National newspapers such as the *New York Times* and the *Chicago Tribune* detailed the action of the feud so far and carried daily revelations of the protagonists' crimes. Members of both families became reluctant national celebrities and the feud itself became legend. Finally, a divided Supreme Court ruled seven to two that Mahon and the others should remain in custody and face trial in Pike County, Kentucky. Of course this meant that they would be brought to justice in the McCoys' home state.

The Final Chapter

By now it was the summer of 1889 and the McCoys' long wait for justice was at an end. After months of legal and constitutional wrangling, the Hatfields were finally going to be tried for their crimes. Even their status as one of the Tug Valley's most prominent and wealthy families had not saved them.

Before the trail even began, Lee Ferguson, the attorney for Pike County, extracted a confession of guilt from Cotton Top

Right: This photograph was taken on September 17, 1907 to celebrate the marriage of Asa Harmon Bud McCoy and Rhoda McCoy.

Left: Bud was the son of Lark and Mary McCoy.

Mounts for the murders of the two McCoy children. Cotton Top also told Ferguson how the three McCoy boys had been kept prisoner at Mate Creek and how they had been shot by Devil Anse, Johnse, Cap, Bill Tom Hatfield, Charles Carpenter, Alex Messer, and Tom Chambers.

Left and Right: Devil Anse's sons Elias and Troy Hatfield. Elias and Troy were murdered by business rival Octavo Gerone on October 17, 1911 in a shootout at Harewood, West Virginia. The Hatfields were saloon owners there. Elias was forty when he died and Troy was thirty-six.

Judge John M. Rice presided over the trial for the three McCoy brothers and handed down life sentences with hard labor to Wall Hatfield, Alex Messer, Dock Mahon, and Plyant Mahon. Known as the "old man" of the gang, Wall Hatfield appealed his sentence but was refused bail and died in prison while he waited for his retrial. Described as being "cool and self-possessed at all times," Wall had petitioned his brothers for help but no one had come to his aid. According to eyewitness accounts, it is highly unlikely that Wall was actually involved in either the murder of the McCoy brothers or the New Year's Massacre.

In a second trial, Cap, Johnse, Robert and Elliott Hatfield, Ellison Mounts, French Ellis, Charles Gillespie, and Thomas Chambers were indicted for the murder of Alifair McCoy on the night of the New Year's Day Massacre. By this time, the rest of the Hatfields were living as fugitives in the mountains of West Virginia. Devil Anse had moved his entire family to a farm in Island Creek, Logan County in 1888 in an effort to distance them from the trouble. The Hatfields were keen to avoid both journalists and the law. It was said that Devil Anse himself was permanently armed with both a rifle and a Colt revolver strapped to his hip. Nine or ten members of his extended family were permanently on guard.

As the trail began, Cotton Top Mounts pleaded guilty to the murder of Alifair McCoy, hoping that he would receive a more lenient sentence. Mounts's lawyer W.M. Connolly soon realized that things were going badly for his client. Sarah McCoy's emotional testimony had obviously had a great effect on the jury. Connolly tried to withdraw Cotton Top's plea, but this was forbidden by Judge Rice.

On August 24, 1889, the jury handed down their sentences. Eight of the defendants received sentences of life imprisonment. (Gillespie was awarded a separate trial but escaped from the Pike County jail and was never brought to justice.) Only Cotton Top Mounts was condemned to hang for his part in the murders. Despite this, no one believed that Ellison's simple son would actually swing; either the Hatfields would break him out of jail, or he would be declared insane. It was also thought likely that Judge Rice would commute his sentence to life imprisonment. But no commutation or escape plan ever materialized. Cotton Top Mounts had been abandoned to his fate.

On February 8, 1890, Cotton Top Mounts was hanged in Pikeville, Kentucky. It was the first hanging in the town for over forty years. Public hanging was illegal by this time, so the fenced-in scaffold was carefully arranged at the bottom of a hill so that the execution was staged in full view of the eight thousand spectators that had gathered to see the grisly spectacle. As the hangman pulled a black hood over poor Cotton Top's head, his last words were "They made me do it! The Hatfields made me do

Following pages: Devil Anse and his wife Levisa stand in front of the tombs of their sons Troy and Elias Hatfield.

Left: Devil Anse and Levisa Hatfield in old age. The respectable-looking couple is photographed in front of the Hatfields' clapboard mansion.

it!" Even at the time, there was a great deal of outrage at the way that the simple-minded Cotton Top was the only man hanged for the murder of the McCoy children. It was widely thought that his incarceration had hastened his mental decay, so that the hangman may have executed a madman.

Arrest warrants remained on file for several Hatfields, including Devil Anse, but no one tried to bring them to justice. It was as though the terrible death of Cotton Top Mounts had finally brought the participants to their senses.

In reality, the two families and their neighbors in the Tug Valley seemed to have grown sick of decades of violence and ill feeling. Cap Hatfield summed up this *entente cordiale* in a letter he wrote to the *Wayne County News* on February 24, 1891. "I do not wish to keep the old feud alive and I suppose that everybody, like myself, is tired of the names of Hatfield and McCoy… we have undergone a fearful loss of noble lives and valuable property in the struggle… Now I propose to rest in a spirit of peace."

The rewards for the capture of the Hatfields were withdrawn and the families decided to keep their distance from each other.

Progress was coming to the Appalachians in the form of the railroad, coal, and lumber. To maximize these opportunities meant stamping out the age-old habit of mountain violence.

Previous pages: The
Hatfields' clapboard
mansion. Devil
Anse and Levisa
Hatfield lived here
in their old age. In
this photograph, the
house is engulfed by
mourners attending
Devil Anse's funeral.

The Aftermath of the Feud

Despite the feuding families' desire for peace, there were still violent ramifications from their decades of hostility.

When the murdered body of Bud McCoy was found in late 1890 it was suspected that his death had been feud-related. Ironically, it turned out that he had been killed by his own relatives Pleasant McCoy and Bill Dyer.

But real feud violence did continue to take place. On May 15, 1890, Dave Stratton was killed in a fit of Hatfield revenge. Stratton had helped Bad Frank Phillips hunt down and murder Jim Vance, the Hatfield uncle who had procured the murder of Asa Harmon McCoy so many years before and had led the New Year's Massacre. Vance's wife found her husband with mortal injuries to his head and chest. He died shortly afterwards. Detective "Kentucky Bill" Napier raised warrants for Devil Anse, Cap, Johnse, and Elliott Hatfield, who were all charged with involvement in Stratton's death. But perhaps the most serious outcome for the family was that a disgusted Governor Fleming withdrew his support and protection from the Hatfields.

The Stratton murder was not the end of Hatfield violence. Although Cap Hatfield had signaled his intention to live in "a spirit of peace" and had become a Methodist in 1894, he was involved in three more shooting deaths in 1897.

Cap and his fourteen-year-old stepson Joseph Glenn came to Matewan, West Virginia during the elections of 1896 and became involved in a shootout with members of the prominent Rutherford family. Cap had had a long-running disagreement with John Rutherford, the son of Matewan mayor Dr. Jim Rutherford, who was also the father-in-law of Floyd McCoy. When the two men met in the town street, they were both drunk. Cap shot and killed both John Rutherford and his nephew Elliott Rutherford. Joe Glenn then shot and killed John's brother-in-law Henderson Chambers to protect his stepfather. The Hatfield pair attempted to escape by railroad but they were captured almost immediately. At their April 1897 trial, Cap and Joe were sentenced to just a year in jail. Even this was too long for Cap, who broke out just three months later in July of that year.

Although there were very few further attempts to bring the Hatfields to justice, Humphrey Ellis did capture Johnse Hatfield in 1898 and brought him in. But Ellis was not destined to enjoy his triumph for long. In July 1899 Elias Hatfield, the eighteen-year-old son of Devil Anse, shot Ellis dead as his train pulled into the town of Gray in Mingo County, West Virginia. Elias himself and his brother Troy Hatfield were subsequently murdered by their business rival Octavo Gerone in Harewood, West Virginia in 1911.

Hatfield violence persisted into the coal field labor troubles of the 1920s. The family became involved on both sides of the

Previous pages: The Hatfields and their supporters gather for Devil Anse's funeral in 1922. Over five thousand people were said to have attended the burial of the famous clan patriarch. His wife Levisa joined him in his magnificent tomb in 1929.

conflict. Logan County Sheriff and Hatfield relative Don Chafin supported the coal mining companies while the Matewan chief of police Sidney "Two-Gun" Hatfield fought for the miners. In the Matewan Massacre of May 19, 1920, the town was the scene of a shootout between the conflicting forces. Eleven men were killed, including town mayor Cabell Testerman who was shot dead by Sid Hatfield.

But most members of both families were keen to leave the feud behind them and take advantage of the economic revival of the Appalachian region.

The Final Years of Devil Anse Hatfield

In a footnote to the violence, clan patriarchs Devil Anse Hatfield and Randall McCoy both survived into their eighties.

Like Randall, Devil Anse turned his back on the fighting. He spent the final years of his life raising hogs on his Island Creek farm in Logan County, West Virginia. He was baptized as a Christian in 1911 but still carried a rifle wherever he went.

In January 1921 Devil Anse suffered a stroke as he sat on his porch with his grandson Joe Caldwell and died of pneumonia on January 6, 1921. He was eighty-one. Joe and Tennis Hatfield commissioned a magnificent Carrera marble tomb complete with a life-sized statue of their father. It was reputed to have cost an enormous three thousand five hundred dollars. Anse's wife joined him there in the tomb in 1929. The monument also bore the names of the couple's thirteen children; Johnson (Johnse), William A. (Cap), Robert L., Nancy, Elliott R., Mary, Elizabeth, Elias, Troy (Detroit), Joseph O., Rose, Willis, and Tennis (Tennyson).

In *The Bluefield Daily Telegraph* of January 8, 1921, Devil Anse was reported to have died the natural death he had always predicted.

The Families are Reconciled

With the deaths of both the Hatfield and McCoy patriarchs and the civilization of the Appalachians, the two families gradually became reconciled to each other. In May 1944 *Life* magazine showed how the American war effort had brought at least two descendants of the families together. Shirley Hatfield and Frankie McCoy both worked in a local factory that produced military uniforms for the troops. The magazine interviewed several other clan members and reported that the two "famous families now live together in peace."

Following pages: The Hatfield family gathers around Devil Anse's open casket at his funeral in 1921. Left to right the funeral goers are Thelma Latelle LaFollett, Mrs Elliott Hatfield, Nancy Hatfield Vance, Rose Hatfield Browning, Levisa Hatfield, Tennis Hatfield, Elliott Mitchel, Elizabeth Hatfield Caldwell, Johnse Hatfield, Smith Hatfield, Emma Smith Elea Hatfield, C.A. Hatfield, Cap Hatfield, Bob Hatfield, Dr. Elliott Hatfield, Murel Hatfield Beres, Joe Wolfe, Ples Browning, and Cook Boys. Devil Anse's funeral was the largest-ever held in Logan County, West Virginia, drawing several thousand people.

Devil Anse Hatfield's Winchester Model 1897 Shotgun

Left: Devil Anse Hatfield poses with his Winchester Model 1897 slide-action shotgun in a "ready to feud" attitude. He also wears two ammunition bandoliers. The lower bandolier is full of Winchester ammunition while the other contains smaller caliber handgun ammunition, probably for his Colt Bisley revolver.

The Winchester Model 1897 was a development of the Winchester Model 1893. The 1893 was an advanced firearm and Winchester's first weapon of this type. It was based on a design by firearms genius John M. Browning. Although thirty five thousand units of the gun were sold between 1893 and 1897, it was only a qualified success. This was mainly because its action could not cope with the new smokeless ammunition, even though it had been designed to do so. The Model 1893 was only produced in twelve-gauge, with two barrel lengths of either thirty- or thirty-

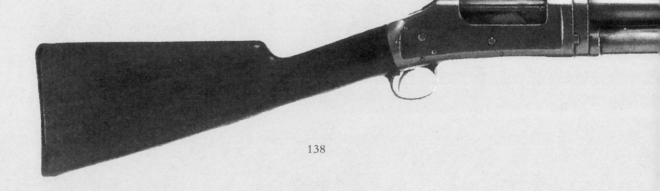

two-inches.

The Model 1983 was soon followed by the much-improved Model 1897. This had a stronger frame and a longer, better-angled stock. It was produced in a variety of models in both twelve- and sixteen-gauge with a variety of barrel lengths between twenty-six and thirty inches. The version shown is a standard Model 1897 in twelve-gauge with a thirty-inch barrel. This appears to be the specification of Devil Anse's gun.

It is significant that the Hatfields did not stint themselves when it came to their weaponry. They usually carried state of the art weapons and liked to be photographed with them. Even a standard Model 1897 cost at least twenty-five dollars, which could rise to a hundred dollars for a checkered and engraved version of the gun.

Above: Devil Anse Hatfield on horseback. He is armed with a Winchester Model 1873 repeating rifle and wears a bandolier of ammunition.

Johnse Hatfield and his Winchester Model 1876

Johnse appears as a fairly young man in this formal studio photograph. He poses with a Winchester repeating rifle, which is probably a Winchester Model 1876. This rifle was a modified version of the Winchester Model 1873. The Model 1873 had become an iconic firearm known as "the gun that won the West." The Model 1876 has a more substantial frame designed to accommodate larger caliber and more powerful centerfire ammunition. Alternatively chambered for 40-60, 45-60, or 50-95 cartridges, the gun was designed to provide the shooter with a large caliber repeating rifle that was suitable for hunting big game, including buffalo.

Theodore Roosevelt, who was famous for his interest in big game hunting, praised the capabilities of the gun. He was photographed wearing his hunting buckskins and coonskin cap and resting a Model 1876 across his knees. The gun proved to be a durable and powerful firearm, but its appeal for Johnse Hatfield probably lay in its brutal stopping power. The gun he is holding appears to be the twenty-eight-inch round-barreled version of

Right: Johnse Hatfield was born on January 6, 1862 in Logan County, West Virginia. He died in Logan County on April 19, 1922.

the Model 1876. This was known as the "Centennial Model" since Winchester released it to celebrate centennial year. Over sixty-four thousand units of this model were manufactured between 1876 and 1897.

The gun had several famous adherents. When Apache warrior Geronimo surrendered in 1886, he was carrying a Model 1876. A carbine version of the gun was also popular.

FAMOUS HATFIELD AND MCCOY DESCENDANTS

The Hatfield and McCoy families went on to have many distinguished descendants. These men and woman have been from many walks of life including politics, music, and business. They also include a well-known fictional character.

Clyde McCoy was a famous jazz trumpet player active in the 1930s and 1940s. Clyde was born in 1903 in Ashland, Kentucky. His famous theme song "Sugar Blues" was released in 1930.

Sidney Hatfield was the famous police chief of Matewan, West Virginia and was a central figure in the Mine Wars of the 1920s. Sidney was the son of Jacob Hatfield and the grandson of the half-brother of Valentine Hatfield. He was gunned down in Welch, West Virginia on August 1, 1921. Hatfield is buried on Radio Hill, just outside the town of Matewan.

Henry Drury Hatfield was the son of Elias Hatfield and the nephew of Devil Anse. He was born in Logan County,

Left: Devil Anse's memorial statue. It was carved from white Carrera marble.

143

Left: Members of
the Hatfield family
pose in front of
Devil Anse's life-size
marble statue. The
statue was erected
by his children. It
was reputed to have
cost three thousand
five hundred dollars.
Devil Anse's wife
Levisa Hatfield is in
the centre of the
photograph.

Left: Devil Anse's nephew Crockett Hatfield and an unknown friend pose with a chained mountain bear. Devil Anse often kept pet bears.

West Virginia in 1875. A Republican, Hatfield was elected the fourteenth governor of West Virginia in 1912. He was elected a United States Senator in 1929 and served until 1935. He died in 1962.

Brian Hatfield is also a politician. A Democrat, he currently serves as a member of the Washington State Senate.

Juliana Hatfield is an Indie rock singer-songwriter and guitarist. Born in 1967 Juliana was a member of the bands *Blake Babies* and *Some Girls* but is now pursuing a solo career. She released a new album *Juliana Hatfield* in 2012.

Football coach Mike D'Antonio also claims to be of Hatfield descent. He was appointed the head coach of the Los Angeles Lakers in November 2012.

Don Blankenship is a member of the McCoy family through his mother. He served as the CEO of Massey Energy, the sixth largest coal company in the United States. Brought up in poverty, he put himself through college by working in the coal mines but grew up to be a self-proclaimed capitalist and Republican.

Leonard "Bones" McCoy was born in 2227, the son of James McCoy. Proud to trace his roots back to the feuding McCoys of earth's nineteenth century, Bones became the chief medical officer of the USS Enterprise in 2266.

The Final Reconciliation

It was not until the twenty-first century that the Hatfield-McCoy feud was finally laid to rest. The Hatfield-McCoy Annual Reunion began in 2000. The tradition was founded by Clyde Floyd "Bo" McCoy Jr. and Sonya Hatfield. Many family members had migrated from the Tug Valley region during the Depression, but returned to the region for this historical gathering. The festivities took place on both sides of the Tug River at Matewan, West Virginia and Pikeville, Kentucky. The reunion went on for three days of feasting and games. These included a family members' marathon and a tug-of-war across the river. The Hatfields wore red ribbons to identify themselves while the McCoys wore blue ribbons.

The Final Ripple

Despite the overwhelming goodwill of most family members towards each other, there was to be a final ripple in the feud. In 2002, Bo and Ron McCoy finally won the right to visit the graves of their ancestors who had died in the feud. The graves are located at the site of the old McCoy farmstead, now on land owned by John Vance. Vance is a descendant of the Hatfield family.

Right: Devil Anse with two unidentified men and a bear in a tree. Devil Anse hunted wild bears and kept them as pets. The two unidentified men could be journalists.

Right: Willis Hatfield. Willis was the twelfth child of Devil Anse and Levisa Hatfield and the younger brother of Johnse Hatfield. A former lawman, Willis led the Hatfield clan at the 1976 Hatfield-McCoy picnic.

Right: A photograph of Frankie McCoy and Shirley Hatfield appeared in *Life* magazine in May 1944. The girls worked in a factory together making military uniforms for the United States army.

The Official Truce

At the fourth reunion held in 2003, sixty descendants of both families signed a truce at Pikeville, Kentucky, led by Reo Hatfield and Bo McCoy. The families maintained that they finally buried their hostilities because of the 9/11 attacks. The ceremony was attended by the governors of West Virginia and Kentucky, Bob Wise and Paul Patton. The families continue to attend the reunions, and 261 family members finished the Hatfield-McCoy marathon in 2012. June 14 has now been proclaimed Hatfield and McCoy Reconciliation Day.

The families now live alongside each other in the Tug Valley. They attend the same schools, sing in the same church choirs, and work the same jobs. The Hatfield-McCoy tourist trail and the annual reunion have become increasingly important to the local economy, bringing visitors and jobs into the region. This income somewhat makes up for the demise of the local coal mining industry.

Left: Three McCoy relatives. Left to right: Syler Branham, J.E. Stanley, and Joe Jack Stanley Jr..

Right: Juliana Hatfield released her solo album *Juliana Hatfield* in 2012.

Opposite page: Senator Brian Hatfield is a Democratic member of the Washington State Senate.

THE HATFIELDS AND THE MCCOYS IN POPULAR CULTURE

Opposite page: The Hatfield-McCoy intersection is located at Matewan, West Virginia.

Below: Samuel Goldwyn produced the 1949 movie *Roseanna McCoy* featuring Joan Evans.

The Hatfield–McCoy feud has captured the American imagination for over one hundred thirty years and continues to fascinate. The feud has woven its way into our popular culture and is reflected in a plethora of books, movies, plays, and television shows. The feud explored mountain honor culture, but also threw light on a wide range of extreme human behavior including violence, madness, romance, lust, betrayal, greed, and revenge. The continuing interest in the feud may be because it reflects the secret dark side of human nature.

THE MIGHTIEST FEUD IN HISTORY··
(THE HATFIELDS AND THE McCOY'S)

SAMUEL GOLDWYN
PRESENTS

Roseanna McCoy

FARLEY GRANGER · CHARLES BICKFORD · RAYMOND MASSEY · RICHARD BASEHART

Screen Play by John Collier

GIGI PERREAU and introducing JOAN EVANS
Distributed by RKO RADIO PICTURES

Directed by IRVING REIS

The Feud in the Movies

The Hatfield-McCoy feud made its first screen appearance in 1923 in Buster Keaton's silent comedy, *Our Hospitality*. The film was a comedy slapstick evocation of the so-called Caulfield-McCay feud.

Samuel Goldwyn produced the 1949 movie *Roseanna McCoy* featuring Joan Evans. The film tells the story of the tragic romance between Roseanna McCoy and Johnse Hatfield. It was not a complete success. A reviewer noted that "the famous mountain families have been satirized and distorted in jokes and comic strips for so many years now that it is difficult to take them seriously."

The Feud on Television

The television movie *The Hatfields and the McCoys* was first aired in 1975. Starring Jack Palance and Steve Forrest as the two clan patriarchs, it ran through the basics of the feuding action.

Somewhat incongruously, the heartbreaking and violent Hatfield-McCoy feud has also been re-interpreted into several cartoons. The first of these appeared in 1950. It was a Warner Brothers' *Bugs Bunny* cartoon where the Martin and McCoy families do some amusing feuding.

Opposite: Buster Keaton was born in 1895 and began performing in vaudeville at the age of three. He went on to become one of the most admired actors and directors in movie history.

Above: Buster Keaton released his silent interpretation of the feud *Our Hospitality* in 1923. It was to be one of his most-enduring films.

In 1964 ABC's animated sitcom *The Flintstones* aired an episode called "The Flintstone Hillbillies" where the Flintstone family feuds with the Hatrocks. Four years later in 1968, Merry Melodies launched the cartoon "Feud with a Dude" where the participants feud over a pig and a chicken.

In a characteristically spooky *Scooby Doo* episode from 1977, the Hatfields feud with the ghost of Old Witch McCoy.

Without a doubt, the most famous television incarnation of

Below: Richard Dawson was born in 1932 and died in June 2012. He was an English-American actor and comedian. He was hired to host *Family Feud* by ABC's game show pioneer Mark Goodson.

165

Left: *Family Feud* first aired on July 12, 1976. It was a breakout hit and Richard Dawson won a Daytime Emmy Award for his work on the show. His habit of kissing the female contestants led to Dawson being nicknamed "the kissing bandit."

Above: Clyde McCoy first launched his album *Sugar Blues* in 1931. It was released by Columbia. He re-worked this material for most of his career. This version was issued in 1951.

Opposite page: The *Star Trek* character Leonard McCoy was first played by DeForest Kelley. Karl Urban took the role in the 2009 *Star Trek* movie.

the Hatfield-McCoy feud is the long-running game show, *Family Feud*. Created by ABC's Mark Goodson and Bill Todman, the first show aired in 1976 and was hosted by Richard Dawson. The unique format of the show brought two feuding families together to compete for cash. In perhaps the most iconic episodes of *Family Feud*, which were televised over the course of a week in 1979, descendants of the Hatfield and McCoy families were brought together to compete for cash prizes. The family members were dressed in hillbilly costumes and the set included a live pig in a wooden cage and dummies dressed in Civil War uniforms. In a reversal of the real feud, the McCoys won the series three games to two. But true to form, the Hatfield family won the most money. *Family Feud* is still on the air, now hosted by comedian Steve Harvey. It is now broadcast in HD.

The most successful ever screen portrayal of the feud itself is History Chanel's 2012 *Hatfields & McCoys* television miniseries. History Chanel first broadcast the show in three two-hour episodes between May 28 and May 30, 2012. The star-studded

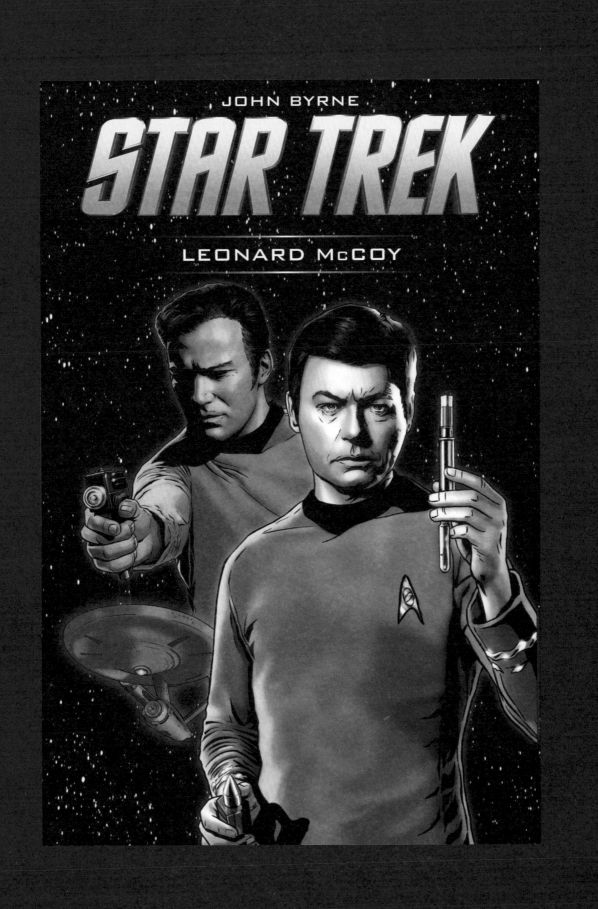

Right:
Hatfields & McCoys was aired in three two-hour episodes between May 28 and May 30, 2012. The miniseries was History channel's first scripted drama.

cast included Kevin Costner as Devil Anse Hatfield, Bill Paxton as Randall McCoy, Lindsay Pulsipher as Roseanne McCoy, Matt Barr as Johnse Hatfield, and Jena Malone as Nancy McCoy. Evocatively shot in rural Romania, the series received many excellent reviews and was described as both "engrossing" and "vivid." The only negative criticism seems to have been reserved for the behavior of the real-life proponents who were described by one reviewer as "bibulous knuckleheads who shot at each other year after year." Another described them as "violent and dull."

Despite this, the show was a huge success. It garnered some of the best ever ratings for a cable television show and was nominated for sixteen awards at the 2012 Primetime Emmy Awards. Kevin Costner won the award for the Outstanding Lead Actor in a Miniseries or a Movie, and Tom Berenger won the category of Outstanding Supporting Actor in a Miniseries or a Movie for his portrayal of a psychopathic Jim Vance.

The miniseries has greatly stimulated interest in the Appalachian Hatfield–McCoy tourist trail. In 2011, the Pigeon Forge resort established the nightly *Hatfields and McCoys Dinner Show,* where the story of the feud is rendered as a musical comedy entertainment.

The feuding families continue to make a contribution to the mountain homeland they both loved.

Randall McCoy's Family Tree

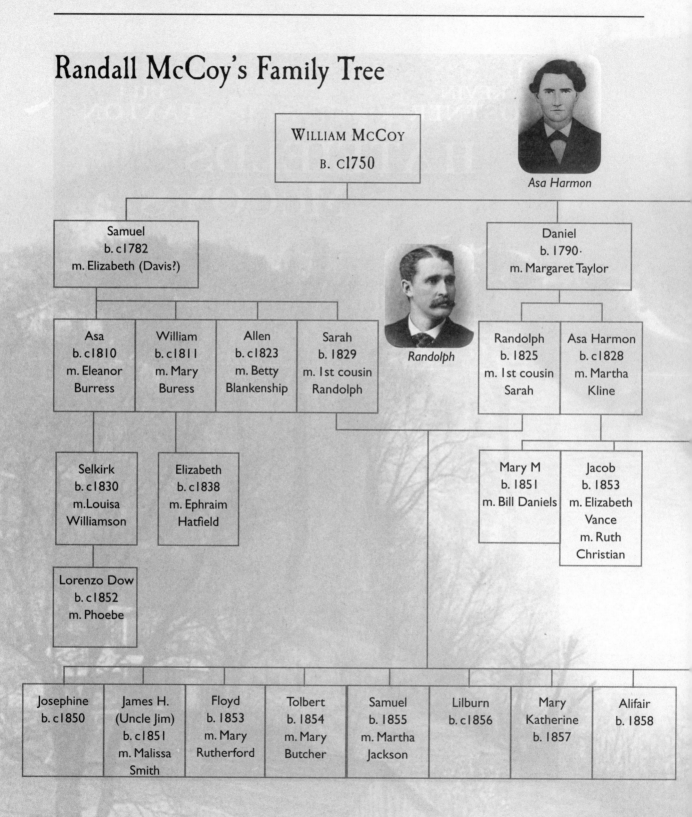

WILLIAM McCOY
B. c1750

Asa Harmon

Randolph

Samuel
b. c1782
m. Elizabeth (Davis?)

Daniel
b. 1790·
m. Margaret Taylor

Asa
b. c1810
m. Eleanor
Burress

William
b. c1811
m. Mary
Buress

Allen
b. c1823
m. Betty
Blankenship

Sarah
b. 1829
m. 1st cousin
Randolph

Randolph
b. 1825
m. 1st cousin
Sarah

Asa Harmon
b. c1828
m. Martha
Kline

Selkirk
b. c1830
m.Louisa
Williamson

Elizabeth
b. c1838
m. Ephraim
Hatfield

Mary M
b. 1851
m. Bill Daniels

Jacob
b. 1853
m. Elizabeth
Vance
m. Ruth
Christian

Lorenzo Dow
b. c1852
m. Phoebe

Josephine
b. c1850

James H.
(Uncle Jim)
b. c1851
m. Malissa
Smith

Floyd
b. 1853
m. Mary
Rutherford

Tolbert
b. 1854
m. Mary
Butcher

Samuel
b. 1855
m. Martha
Jackson

Lilburn
b. c1856

**Mary
Katherine**
b. 1857

Alifair
b. 1858

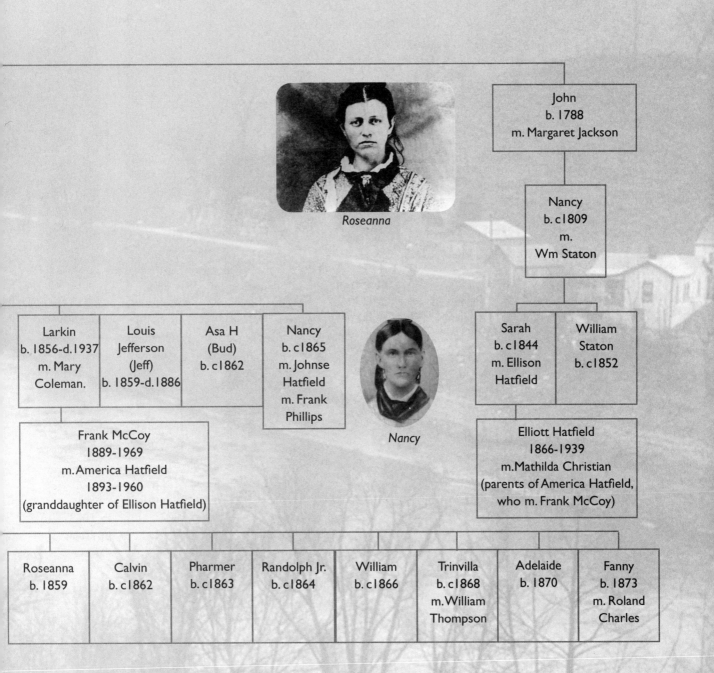

Roseanna

John
b. 1788
m. Margaret Jackson

Nancy
b. c1809
m.
Wm Staton

Larkin
b. 1856-d.1937
m. Mary
Coleman.

Louis
Jefferson
(Jeff)
b. 1859-d.1886

Asa H
(Bud)
b. c1862

Nancy
b. c1865
m. Johnse
Hatfield
m. Frank
Phillips

Nancy

Sarah
b. c1844
m. Ellison
Hatfield

William
Staton
b. c1852

Frank McCoy
1889-1969
m. America Hatfield
1893-1960
(granddaughter of Ellison Hatfield)

Elliott Hatfield
1866-1939
m. Mathilda Christian
(parents of America Hatfield,
who m. Frank McCoy)

Roseanna
b. 1859

Calvin
b. c1862

Pharmer
b. c1863

Randolph Jr.
b. c1864

William
b. c1866

Trinvilla
b. c1868
m. William
Thompson

Adelaide
b. 1870

Fanny
b. 1873
m. Roland
Charles

Devil Anse Hatfield's Family Tree

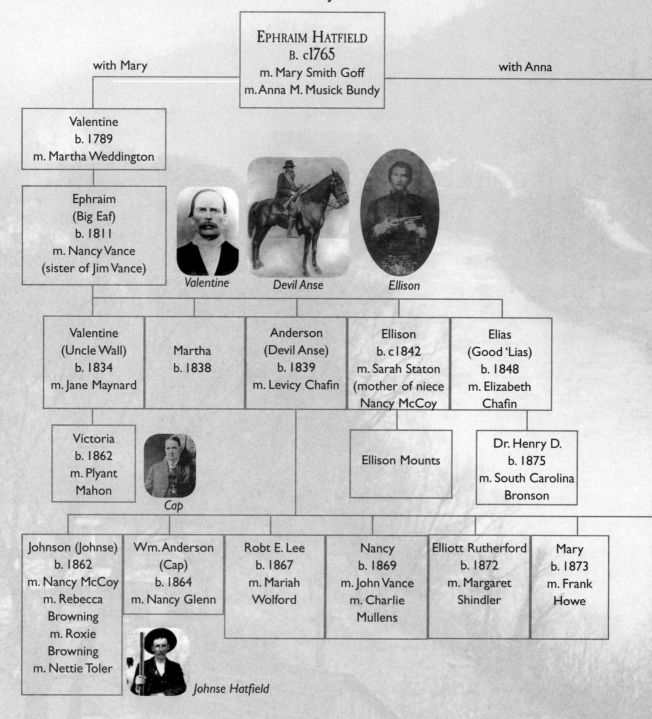

EPHRAIM HATFIELD
B. c1765
m. Mary Smith Goff
m. Anna M. Musick Bundy

with Mary

with Anna

Valentine
b. 1789
m. Martha Weddington

Ephraim
(Big Eaf)
b. 1811
m. Nancy Vance
(sister of Jim Vance)

Valentine

Devil Anse

Ellison

Valentine
(Uncle Wall)
b. 1834
m. Jane Maynard

Martha
b. 1838

Anderson
(Devil Anse)
b. 1839
m. Levicy Chafin

Ellison
b. c1842
m. Sarah Staton
(mother of niece
Nancy McCoy

Elias
(Good 'Lias)
b. 1848
m. Elizabeth
Chafin

Victoria
b. 1862
m. Plyant
Mahon

Cap

Ellison Mounts

Dr. Henry D.
b. 1875
m. South Carolina
Bronson

Johnson (Johnse)
b. 1862
m. Nancy McCoy
m. Rebecca
Browning
m. Roxie
Browning
m. Nettie Toler

Wm. Anderson
(Cap)
b. 1864
m. Nancy Glenn

Robt E. Lee
b. 1867
m. Mariah
Wolford

Nancy
b. 1869
m. John Vance
m. Charlie
Mullens

Elliott Rutherford
b. 1872
m. Margaret
Shindler

Mary
b. 1873
m. Frank
Howe

Johnse Hatfield

George
b. 1804
m. Nancy Whitt

Jeremiah
b. 1805
m. Rachel Vance

Anderson
(Deacon Anse)
b. 1835
m.
Polly Runyan

Basil
b. c1840
m.
Nancy Lowe

Elias
(Bad 'Lias)
b. 1853
m. Jane Chafin

Floyd
b. 1858
m. Anne Pinson
m. Jenny Hunt

Ephraim
b. 1838
m. Elizabeth
McCoy

Jacob
b. 1843/45
m. Rebecca
Crabtree

William Sidney
(Two-Gun Sid)
b. 1891/93
m. Jessie Lee
Testerman (née
Maynard)

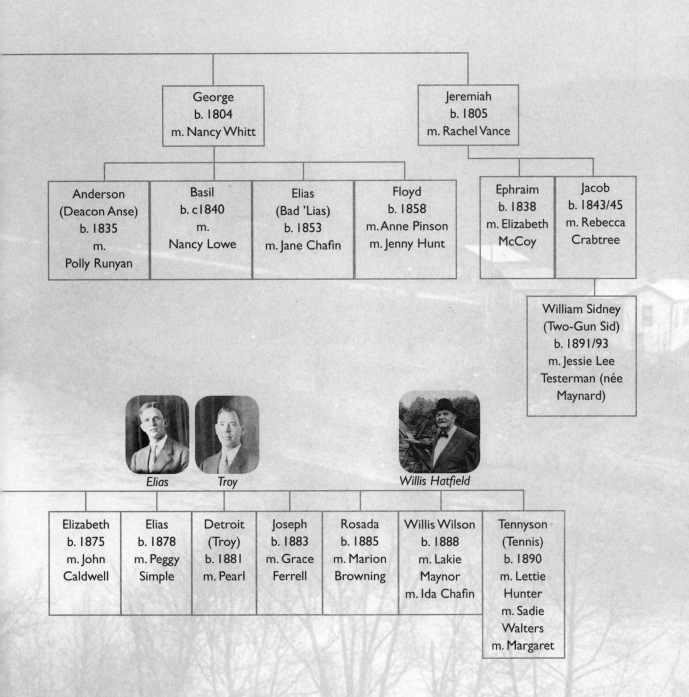

Elias   *Troy*   *Willis Hatfield*

Elizabeth
b. 1875
m. John
Caldwell

Elias
b. 1878
m. Peggy
Simple

Detroit
(Troy)
b. 1881
m. Pearl

Joseph
b. 1883
m. Grace
Ferrell

Rosada
b. 1885
m. Marion
Browning

Willis Wilson
b. 1888
m. Lakie
Maynor
m. Ida Chafin

Tennyson
(Tennis)
b. 1890
m. Lettie
Hunter
m. Sadie
Walters
m. Margaret

Acknowledgments

The publisher and author would like to thank the following for their help in producing this book:

Debra A. Basham, the records archivist of the West Virginia State Archives, for the archive photographs.

Eric Douglas for the Hatfield Cemetery images.

Patrick F. Hogan at the Rock Island Auction Co. for the firearms images.